TALES OF THE MOHAWKS

by

Alma Greene
(Gah-wonh-nos-doh/Forbidden Voice)

Illustrations
by

R. G. Miller

J. M. DENT & SONS (CANADA) LIMITED

This book is set in Baskerville 10/10 and 11/13 type
The paper stock is 70 lb. opaque litho

Printed in Canada

1 2 3 4 5 6 7 8 9 10 Alg 84 83 82 81 80 79 78 77 76 75

CONTENTS

BEGINNINGS

Before the white civilization came to the Western Hemisphere, the land was inhabited by the Natives of America. They had everything to make them happy and walked hand in hand with nature, which provided a cure for every pain. When winter came upon them, the Natives had already gathered and stored from the woods all the things they would require.

The Native people were very happy to live in a world created by the Great Spirit, unpolluted by sin. It was very important for them to use the Sacred Tobacco to give thanks to the Creator and to the spirits of the roots and herbs, which would then give forth their healing powers.

 In the evening the Native people sat on the ground in a semi-circle in front of a huge crackling fire, listening to the tales narrated by the elders of their tribe and handed down from generation to generation.

Even today the Native people are tireless story-tellers. They pass on the legends of bygone days, and like the people of old, they also tell stories of things that have happened to them or their friends.

OHKWAHO

In the beginning there was no land. One day the creatures who dwelt in the water heard a voice saying that a young maiden who was to become a mother was going to be sent down to live with them.

The creatures held a conference. The turtle suggested that the maiden could land on his back, as he was big and could remain quiet and steady. Various things gathered around the turtle, and gradually a large piece of land with trees and shrubs was formed. Thus the maiden had a comfortable place where she could live.

One day while out walking, the maiden heard voices. They seemed to be arguing about something. She listened and heard the voices again. They came from her unborn babies. One was restless and quarrelsome; the other was kind and gentle.

The restless one said he was tired of being confined and wanted to force his birth. The other told him to wait and have patience, as they had a mission to carry out. The restless child refused to listen and at that moment forced his birth. This resulted in the mother's death.

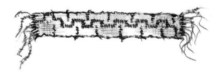

After many years, the place had become inhabited by Natives. However, something was wrong. The people were restless and quarrelsome, and abnormal babies were being born. Old people had dreams warning of some unknown disaster.

At night the forest echoed with the sounds of dogs howling. A wise old owl sat in a tree, desperately trying to tell someone what he knew. Night after night he cried, 'I know, I know, I know.'

One night an old lady had a dream. She knew it must, in some way, explain the unhappiness and sorrow among the Native tribes.

In her dream she saw a young maiden about to give birth to twin boys. The mother said she had heard arguments from her unborn babies: one said he would cause people to fight with one another, as it was the only way he would thrive in this world; the other baby told his brother to be patient, for they had an important mission on earth.

The old lady went to a wise man about her dream. This is what he told her: 'In a short while a little girl will become ill. Watch her closely and listen carefully to her dying words. In this way the Nation will be saved.'

Soon after, the old lady heard of this child's illness. The little girl was pleading for someone to lash her with a red whip, to punish her for disobeying her parents when she was well.

The old lady who had had the dream went to see this little girl, who was still moaning for someone to lash her. The old lady told the parents that if they wanted to see their only child rest in peace and if they wanted to redeem themselves for the sin of not correcting her behaviour, they must comply with the child's last wishes.

And so they went out and cut four tiny red whips from the woods. They returned and went in to stand beside the bed. The child's eyes were wild and pleading. Everyone was sent out of the room. The father stepped forward and, with tears streaming down his face, lashed his dying baby. Slowly she quieted down. He then gave the red whips to his wife, who repeated the lashing.

The child went into a convulsion and let out a most horrifying scream. As she died, something could be seen to run through her body like a flash of lightning.

The Natives said it was the restless baby who had hurried his birth and thus killed his mother. He was full of evil, and the Natives named him Flint.

THE TREE OF PEACE

The Tree of Peace was the law of the Confederacy and stood for love and justice between individuals and nations.

The Eagle-that-sees-far was placed on the very top of the Tree of Peace to signify watchfulness and to watch over the roots which extend to the north, south, east and west. The Eagle will discover if any evil approaches the Confederacy and shall warn them.

DYAONHRONHKO

THE WEST WIND

An Indian maiden, close to marriageable age, was reminded by her parents of the traditions of her ancestors. The parents would look for a suitable husband, and when they found one they would purchase five yards of the finest cotton and present it to the future husband's parents. If it was kept by them, the daughter was accepted, and the two families could begin marriage preparations at once.

The Indian maiden was not happy with her parents' choice and asked them for a little time. She knew she would have to obey them

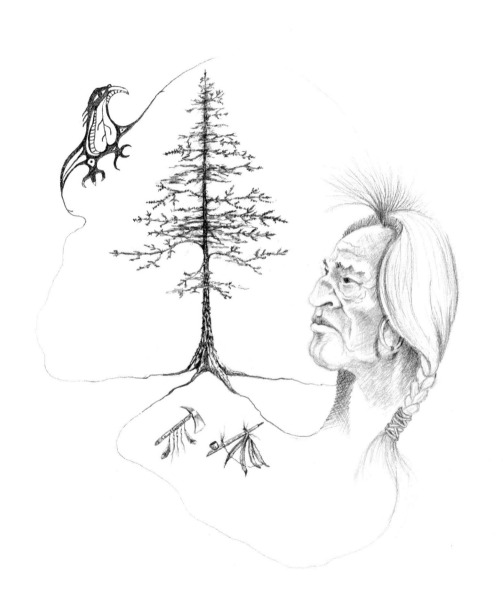

in this matter, but she did not love the man and did not want to marry him.

The girl went for a walk to think about her situation. Suddenly she heard a voice, but looking around could not see anyone. It could only be the wind. But again she heard a voice saying: 'Choose; take me. I love you very much.'

The voice grew louder, calling, 'Take me — I love you.' This time she called back, 'Who are you? I cannot see you; how can I marry you?' The wind wailed again, 'Marry me, marry me. I am the West Wind, and I will die if you do not marry me.'

Slowly the West Wind sighed to a halt. Suddenly the birds stopped singing; the sun darkened, the waters stopped flowing and the trees whispered, 'Oh, Indian maiden, marry him.' And the hills and bushes echoed, 'Marry him.'

The maiden's heart was touched, and she cried out: 'Oh, West Wind, do not die; I love you; I will marry you.'

The West Wind and the Indian maiden were married by the Great Thunder, who was wise and knew what was happening all over the world. There was a great feast, and everyone danced with happiness for the married couple.

Then the Thunder spoke in a loud voice to all the people attending the wedding. 'Listen to me,' he said. 'There is one more thing left for us to do. We have witnessed a fine marriage. The maiden has been a loving daughter; her heart is sincere and pure and she is full of compassion.'

The Thunder gave three loud claps. The third clap caused beautiful fireworks. When the clouds drifted away, a handsome Indian brave was standing in front of the maiden.

A wicked witch had turned this young man into the West Wind, and it was the maiden's love which had broken the curse. The Indian brave kissed his beautiful bride and told her he had watched over and loved her for many years. There was great rejoicing, and the couple was showered with gifts.

In the second year of their marriage, the Indian brave and his lovely wife became the parents of a little boy called Hiawatha.

Long before the coming of the white man, the ancient tribes had fallen into a savage state and warred continually one against another. Then the Creator-who-sees-all-things sent the Good Message to his people. He wanted them to know there was a Hereafter but they could not expect to go there if they continued to behave as they were doing.

This is how the message came to the people: A sentry going his rounds saw a man by a fire. The man told the sentry he was the One-that-always-was and had been sent from above. His face glowed with light. The warrior did not understand what he saw and heard, but he carried the tale to the Mohawk settlement.

Around the Council Fire it was decided that if the stranger could prove himself, the people would listen to his message. The stranger, who was called Daganawida, agreed to the conditions.

The people had Daganawida climb a tree, then they cut it down, and he fell into a deep chasm with a wild stream at the bottom. Daganawida made a stone canoe and by his divine power was able to float to safety in it. The Native people again saw the smoke of his fire and knew he had survived the ordeal.

The chiefs accepted the message of peace and goodwill and agreed that the fighting between tribes should stop. Daganawida planted a tree, then he knocked it over. Under the tree was a great hole filled with gushing waters, and the Native warriors threw all their weapons into the hole.

The Mohawk chief Hiawatha became Daganawida's helper, and the two together ordained the Chiefs of the Confederacy, even including Atotarho, the wizard and chief of the Onondagas. The Five Nations of the Confederacy (and a sixth which was admitted later) remain joined in brotherhood to this day.

FAIRY RINGS

In the beginning, the Natives of America lived in common with the Little People (Ya-go-de-noh-yoh-yahs) and Witches (Ro-nut-gonh). Everybody lived in harmony, as these two societies worked together for the good of their people.

The fairies, or Little People, were blessed with supernatural powers, and they vested these only in people who were in trouble yet faithful in their own tribal beliefs.

The Witches were blessed with a divine knowledge of roots and herbs for curing people's ailments. They always followed a special ritual before gathering the medicine.

Another person could sometimes help cure a patient. This person is called Deh-ha-de-ya-do-reh-tha, or Fortune-teller. Even today, when there is sickness in the home, along with unusual happenings and unexplained noises, a Fortune-teller is consulted. No money is required to pay for the services of these talented people. Their powers depend on tribal belief and are held sacred.

TAWISTAWIS

The young Indian girl was alone when it happened. All the people of her tribe had gone in search of a new location for a settlement. Tears streamed down her cheeks as she realized that her baby would be born with no one to help her.

She screamed out in agony to the moon and to the stars, and great beads of moisture formed on her brow. Once more she looked up to the heavens. However, it was not the stars she saw, but multitudes of people, little people skipping down the golden stairs which led to her own door, illuminating the room with a radiance she had never seen before.

At that instant she forgot her pain, as a strange feeling came over her and she felt the touch of cool hands on her brow. Someone was saying, 'We have been watching you for many nights. We have suffered the agonies of your pain and we have come to help you. You do not know who we are or how we come to be here.

'We are the Little People, called Ya-go-de-noh-yoh-yahs (fairies), which means we live in the crevices of rocks. Not many people have seen us. We also have one brother called Deh-ha-ronh-ya-ga-nel-reh, meaning he walks upon the earth and reaches the skies. He is taller than the highest Oneh-da-Gowah (pine tree). He has a great mission; blessed is he who sees him.

'We are supernatural and our mission is to perform good deeds for the poor and humble. We appear in the dreams of the Onh-gwe-honh-weh (Indian) to warn them of approaching danger. We have a way to help people in trouble. We play and dance in the moonlight, our clothes are spun from the mists of heaven, and even though they cannot see us, we guard the Natives from all harm and danger.

'We are here because you are soon to give birth to your baby, and we need another star to add to our flock. It shall be your decision to let her go and become one of us Ya-go-de-noh-yoh-yahs. She can see you every day, and you will know where she is, for she is a part of you and you of her.

'Now, you will sleep and make your decision, and the new day will bring you peace and happiness.'

And so a new fairy was born.

CRYSTAL BALL

There are many crystal balls in the world, but there is only one which is given by the Little People who live in the crevices of rocks. This crystal ball is used only for good purposes and can be held only by a person with a pure heart. It will reveal the perplexities of a life and tell how to combat them. In time of illness, it will reveal the cause, source and cure.

The Witches' Crystal Ball is obtained from some evil source for the price of one's soul. This crystal ball is very powerful and dangerous.

One day many years ago, a young man went walking in the woods. He was very troubled. He was engaged to be married to a nice girl, whom he loved very much. Now she had disappeared, leaving a note saying, 'Sorry, you are not the one; do not look for me.'

He was very unhappy. As he walked he came upon an old man with a white beard sitting on a fallen tree. The old gentleman took the man's hand and asked him to sit down beside him, saying that he knew all about the man's worries. Then the old gentleman told the man that he had been waiting for him because he was a good man and should never be hurt.

The young man said he wanted to know about his lost love, so the old man gave him a crystal ball and told him that before he looked into it he must put all his thinking capacity to what he wanted to know.

The young man looked into the crystal ball and saw his sweetheart going from him to another man. He saw a broken marriage, with the woman and her little children looking in vain for happiness.

He bowed his head for a second, then standing erect, he gave the crystal ball back to the old man and thanked him for this timely revelation.

The old man smiled and said, 'Son, you have proven worthy. I have no heirs to give the crystal ball to, so I will give it to you with all my blessings. Take it and use it wisely.'

The old man vanished from sight, but the crystal ball is still on the Indian settlement, and it has helped many people.

PURIFICATION DANCE

The fairies, or Little People, had a party one night. It was the occasion for each fairy to report her good deeds, and before the meeting was called to order, all the fairies joined hands and danced on the moonbeams. High up on the Milky Way, Flint and the bad fairy sat plotting and planning their next move.

It was no longer safe to go walking in the forest. Little children came home crying because they had been chased by a roaring lion, which called to them in a human voice. It was the work of either Flint or the bad fairy.

The bad fairy had a magic wand which could do all manner of things, such as transform people into objects or animals. However, she had no power over Flint. He liked evil people and children who disobeyed their parents.

It was in the spring, when the Natives of the Mohawk tribe begin planting their corn. The head of each family brought a portion of the sacred tobacco and placed it in a large bucket for the thanksgiving ceremony to the Great Spirit. This ritual always preceded the planting season.

The men, women and children gathered around the fire, and the ceremony began with the thanksgiving prayer. The spokesman threw the sacred tobacco upon the dying embers; a black cloud rose and then descended, covering the group which had gathered around the fire.

An old chief stood up and spoke to his people: 'Something has gone wrong. Someone is here who is not pure of heart.' It was Flint and the bad fairy who had caused the black cloud, but their mischief was to be short-lived.

The chief rose once more. Beckoning his people, he led them round and round the dying embers in a slow rhythm, following most solemnly the traditions of his ancestors. This was the purification dance of the Mohawks.

Suddenly a little girl clapped her hands and pointed to the fire, crying: 'The Little People, the fairies; they have cleansed the fire with the stroke of their wand.'

The people kept on dancing around the fire until the smoke arose to the heavens above. The old chief told his people to make preparation for the evening. They must respect and thank their friends, the Little People, for looking after them.

That night the people came in large numbers, bringing dainty delicacies — a pot of the traditional corn soup, cookies moulded to represent little dolls, bracelets made out of corn kernels coloured in the juice of elderberry, and tiny little moccasins, the emblem of good luck. A spokesman performed the ceremony, and the people danced the dance of the Little People, keeping rhythm to the water drums. Just before daybreak, a warm breeze began to blow, bringing peace and goodwill to all.

The old chief spoke once more. He told them that they had just witnessed the power of evil. They must never forget the teachings of their fathers. They must also remember that they are parents of innocent children, who are here on earth as visitors from heaven and must hear only golden words of wisdom from their parents. Only then shall the parents be rewarded. He then turned to the children, saying: 'You must obey your parents, as they are sent by the Great Spirit to guide your steps along the way. This life will surely end, and it is only love which prevails against evil here on earth.'

Flint and the wicked fairy delighted to get into the homes of families and create a commotion. They accomplished many things to make people unhappy.

Then Flint had a new idea. He knew the Native people were superstitious and on account of this were easily disturbed. So one night at midnight he went to the place where horses were kept and captured a black colt. He braided the mane and tail of the colt and let it go back with the rest of the horses.

Early the next morning the black colt was discovered by the owner. The people were greatly disturbed. When the same thing happened the next two mornings, the families drew close together and would not allow their children to go too far away.

The leaders of the settlement held a conference and decided that evil spirits were at work. They knew about Flint and the wicked fairy and that they could be anywhere and do anything.

The good fairies also held a conference to counteract the activities of Flint and the wicked fairy. They decided on a plan.

Early the next morning one of the fairies, dressed in ordinary clothes, offered to read the fortune of the owner of the colt. She told him that what was happening was the work of Flint and that he should follow her advice.

She gave him a round stone, a little larger than an apple, and told him it was magic and would obey its master. He must go alone to a secluded place and say the magic words to command the stone, and then he must bury three kernels of corn in the ground. This he must do each time he wanted the stone to do something for him. This stone would be his luck-charm and would remain in his family for all time to come.

The fairy said that she had already told the stone what to do and that the man must now take it and set it up on the post beside the gate which led to the pasture.

That evening when Flint went back to the pasture he could see something on the gate-post. As he drew nearer he saw it was a skull, with bright lights coming from its eye sockets. Its bony mouth was quivering, and it was muttering, 'Run, Flint, run while you can. Run, Flint, you've had your fun.'

Flint was so frightened he just stood and stared, thinking of the time when he himself would be only a skull. He ran to his hiding place, and that is where the wicked fairy found him many days later.

The owner of the horse was happy, for he now owned a luck-charm which would protect his family for all time to come.

THE BABY AND THE CURSE

There was great rejoicing in the community when a beautiful baby was born to two fine people who had been married for twenty-five years. The old ladies in the community said they would have a celebration in honour of the event and invite all the Little People (fairies). This was a traditional rite, and so a proclamation was issued.

When Flint and the wicked fairy heard about the new baby, they hurried to disguise themselves as good fairies and rushed over to see the new baby. The parents received them most graciously and let them hold the baby.

Flint and the wicked fairy cast a spell on the baby: she would never talk nor make any sound until the spell was broken. The parents did not know about the curse, and preparation for the celebration continued.

On the night of the party the fairies, in gay sparkling attire, stood in line to hold the baby and bestow upon her all the grace and talent only the fairies could give. Friends and kind neighbours brought many gifts, and there was great rejoicing.

As time went on the baby became lovelier. She never cried when upset. When it was time for her to talk, she tried to speak but could utter no sound.

It was the child's third birthday. The parents were greatly concerned about their daughter's condition and decided to have a party for her, hoping that new interests would encourage her to talk.

The good fairies warned the parents to keep the child hidden from people until the time of the party. The fairies would then take over, and whatever was wrong would be corrected. The fairies were certain that Flint had been up to more of his tricks. They knew the little girl was under a curse but were not sure what the curse was.

At the party the fairies brought all sorts of objects to attract the little girl's attention, but to no avail. Then they brought in a caged reptile. Everyone gasped and looked on in horror, but the little girl held out both hands to caress it. The fairies assured the parents that they need not worry; their baby would not be harmed.

A fairy waved her wand over the reptile; it coiled up and went to sleep. Slowly she opened the cage. The baby crawled towards the reptile, clapping her hands. Suddenly she laughed out loud. Then she lay down beside the animal and went to sleep.

The parents were very happy that the baby could now laugh and talk. The curse of Flint was broken forever.

A VISIT TO FAIRYLAND

A little girl, whose name was Sandy, was happy with her parents. She had no playmates except the animals and birds she met in the woods. However, her mother never worried about her when she roamed through the woods, as she had confidence in the fairies, who had promised to watch over her.

One morning after she had her milk and porridge, Sandy went into the woods to play. The birds and all the animals flocked around her, saying: 'Come play with us.'

On and on they went, skipping and jumping, until they came to a huge door. The butterfly knocked on the door; they all waited patiently, and someone said, 'Who is there?'

They looked up to see where the voice had come from, and towering high above their heads was a Giraffe. He opened the door to let them in. The Giraffe, who was the doorkeeper, gave them a warm welcome. Sandy went in, followed by her friends: frogs, reptiles, raccoons, squirrels, rabbits, dogs, cats and cows. It was beautiful behind the door, like stepping into another world.

The Giraffe rang a bell, which brought the cook, a large, motherly Elephant. The Giraffe said to the Elephant: 'We have guests. You know the golden rule: food before pleasure. We shall listen for the dinner gong.'

He told his guests they were at liberty to explore his kingdom. The animals elected Sandy to be their leader. They went into one room and found a swing made of multicoloured climbing roses with a swing board of solid gold. Sandy rocked back and forth to the music of a lullaby once sung to her by her mother.

Sandy and the animals entered another room. Here the ceiling, walls and floor were made of mirrored glass, in which they could all see themselves. Sandy stood in front of a mirror. She felt content and liked the way she smiled. She thought of her loving parents and fell to her knees in prayer, wishing all children could have such loving parents. She looked in the mirror again and saw upon her head a crown of roses, which filled the room with their fragrance.

In a corner of the mirror room was the fountain of wisdom. At a certain time each day, every living creature who visited the room was fulfilled, each according to his needs.

No other human being had ever seen this underground enchanted palace. Sandy was the first. For a second time she sat on the swing, deep in thought. Suddenly she was aroused by the ringing of bells meaning that lunch was being served.

The dining area was long, large and with many different-sized tables. The mice had a low table decorated with cheese in the form of flowers. The big cats and the other animals of the same size had a higher table, a glass of ice-cold milk beside each setting. The birds had an oval-shaped table with a white porcelain trough around it filled with delicious bird-seed.

Before the lunch began, Sandy stood, face uplifted, with her eyes closed and hands clasped, and asked blessing for the food. As she sat down, the birds broke into a strain of heavenly music.

It was getting late and was time for Sandy to return home. However, there was one more room she had to see. Sandy and her friends opened the door to this room. It was dimly lit, and the music they heard only angels could sing. The strains of this music slowly left the room, leaving only the echoes of peace.

They looked around and saw skeletons perched on poles across the room. They were skeletons of birds and other creatures, once filled with life given by the Creator. Children and grown-ups had committed the deed of destruction on them, and there was not one that fell to the ground to be left unnoticed. Each one was tenderly lifted and taken to the morgue of this underground palace. These creatures who had been so cruelly destroyed sang every day for the forgiveness of the cruelty of man.

FORBIDDEN ROOM

A man and his wife were heirs to a large, century-old house, situated near an Indian settlement. The present owner of the house was very ill. He felt he would not live very much longer, so he called in this couple. Certain obligations had to be fulfilled before they could assume ownership; if these conditions were met, the old man would turn over the house to them. The man and his wife agreed.

The sick man was satisfied with the couple's co-operation and began to tell them some of the mysteries surrounding the house. His great-grandfather had originally bought the house from an Egyptian. The Egyptian told his great-grandfather that there was one room in the house which must never be opened. The Egyptian then signed all the documents and handed over the key to the room. That same night he died.

The house was handed down to its present owner, and he now signed the necessary documents and gave the keys to the young couple. The house was theirs.

Unfortunately, it was only a few short years before the man's wife, along with their child, died during childbirth. The man, overwhelmed with grief, decided to stay in the house alone. Time passed, and he grew curious about the forbidden room.

One day he got the key to this room and went upstairs. The door to the room was the same as the other doors in the house. He turned the key and opened the door. It was an attractive room. The furniture was of Egyptian design, and the wallpaper was most unusual. The man was fascinated. On the wallpaper were trees, a stream and life-like pictures of beautiful girls with wings.

As he stood admiring the wallpaper, the man heard water running and felt a breeze blowing. Surprisingly, it was the stream on the wallpaper that was flowing, and the trees on it were being blown from side to side. Even the beautiful girls were stretching out their arms to him. Puzzled, he left the room and spent a sleepless night thinking about what he had seen.

The next day he took all the furniture and pictures out of the room. He examined each item carefully and could find nothing unusual. As he had found no clues, he decided to return to the room. He was inside for only a few minutes when he heard the same things — water running, trees swaying in the breeze and the lovely girls pleading for help. He backed out of the room and locked the door.

In the morning, he decided what to do. He went into the city and brought home new paper for the forbidden room. He began to

27

tear the old paper off the walls. The waters stood still; the trees stopped swaying, and the girls with wings remained still.

As he pulled the paper, the man discovered something attached to the wall. It was a document printed in foreign characters. He removed it carefully and took it to the local authorities to see if it could be translated. The only person able to translate it was a doctor who lived in Egypt, so this man went off in search of him.

This is how the learned doctor translated the document:

'A long time ago, the Egyptian's magic came into conflict with the fairies' magic wands. The wands would be saved if they remained together, or in a group. However, one day one fairy was found alone in the woods, and the Egyptian who had owned the old house conquered her power. Thus, all the fairies were imprisoned underneath the wallpaper.'

For years there were no fairies in the land. The inscription declared that the spell would be broken only by someone who disobeyed the traditions of the old house and removed the wallpaper. And so the spell was broken, and the fairies were liberated.

WITCHES' BREW

The Natives believe that a person who practises witchcraft is in league with the devil. This belief was introduced to the Six Nations by the Algonquin tribe.

There are two methods employed by witches to accomplish their ends. One is by suggestion, either verbal or telepathic. Witches who practise this method are able to assume the form of ancient monsters, the bear being the favourite form. They have the power to transform people into beasts and to imprison them within trees without destroying their human nature.

Witches of the other class work their spells by introducing into the body of their victim, by supernatural means, a small, needle-like splinter, pointed on both ends and having a central eye to which is tied a hair of the witch. When the victim is looked after by a good witch, these splinters can be drawn out with a witch poultice. When the witch's needle is pulled out, it can be reversed and sometimes the evil witch dies.

To burn the object withdrawn from a victim means torture to the witch and in the end causes death. Sometimes the object, once withdrawn, can be thrown through space to injure the witch whenever desired.

Witch poison may be extracted by putting finely sifted ashes on the afflicted part of the victim, who must stay in bed until the poison comes out. The witch's charm will then be found in the ashes. When a victim dies of a great witch's charm, the spirit of the witch is able to return to the corpse before burial and repossess its medicine.

Witches fear the threat of an angry person's desire to kill them. This fear acts as a charm against further annoyance.

To torture a witch, so as to force a confession and a promise of repentance, it is necessary to take a living blackbird, carry it into the woods at midnight, build a fire and then split open the bird's body. Take out its beating heart and hang it by its cords over a slow fire. The witch is conscious of what is going on and does her best to reach the spot and beg that the heart be taken from the fire before it is consumed. At this point you can get anything from the witch. She is only too willing to confess, even to repent of her evil ways. If the heart is consumed by the slow fire, the witch will die of a burnt heart.

OKWARI

MAN-EATING PLANT

There was trouble in the camp of the witches. The serpent, who was the head of all witches, had been humiliated by his cousin the black worm, who was always trying to be smarter than the serpent and was feared by everybody.

The black worm created trouble among the Natives. He caused illness and created unsightly objects which terrified the people. The old serpent warned the black worm that if he did not act like the rest of the witches he would be punished.

The black worm defied the serpent by making him very ill. The serpent was furious. He laid a trap for the worm and had just nicely finished when the black worm slipped right into it.

The black worm was helpless and could only move his head. He was so angry he could not think of anything but revenge, and he had so much witch power that he could do much harm. Finally, he decided on a plan. He knew that every time he spat on the ground a man-eating plant would spring up, and he thought that when he got enough of these plants they would break his chains and release him.

At last he had a collection of plants, and they were devouring all the insects. The old serpent did not dare go into the woods. Soon there were so many man-eating plants in the woods that there was no more wild game for the Natives to hunt.

But the black worm was in trouble too. There were many poisonous plants and not enough living creatures to satisfy them all, and the plants were about to eat the black worm.

Knowing his difficult and dangerous situation, the worm began sending messages to his cousin, the serpent. When the serpent received the first message, he summoned all the witches for a conference.

The witches knew that if nothing was done about these plants, everybody would be destroyed. They decided that they had to save the Natives from destruction.

The serpent told the worm that he had broken all the rules in the witch kingdom. He said that the witches had had a meeting and decided they would give the black worm one last chance to change his ways. If he refused, the witches would take drastic steps.

The black worm said he could make his own decisions and would act accordingly.

The witches called for a last convention. They had just heard that an innocent girl had been devoured by the plants, and they were very unhappy with this news. They knew that the black worm would never change his ways and that if they liberated him there would only be more trouble. There was much evil in witchcraft, and so they made a final resolution that all witchcraft would have to be destroyed.

All the witches at the convention took their medicine into the woods to be set on fire at midnight. At the hour of midnight, fires were started all around the edge of the woods so that nothing could escape. The fire lasted for three days, and the black worm screamed right to the end, but that was the only way the man-eating plants could be destroyed.

The Native settlement was cleared of witches for many years, and the people lived in love and harmony with one another.

THE IMPRINT

A well-known woman became very ill. Each night a large strange dog would stand and look in at her window. This caused her suffering throughout the night. When this woman was near death, she called her people to her bedside. She told them that she knew they did not believe in witchcraft, but there was one thing she wanted them to do. She told them to turn her on her side when she had taken her last breath. They would see the imprint of a hand in black on her back. When the woman died, her wishes were followed, and indeed, the imprint was seen on her back.

A woman suspected of being a witch went to see the deceased woman. The next day when they dressed the woman for the funeral the imprint had disappeared.

THE EMPTY POT

One time a witch let her pot get empty. Thus she was required to destroy the one she most loved or give herself to the devil. She began to plot and plan.

She decided to kill a rabbit and use its blood to replenish her pot. Two weeks later she would attend the meeting of the witch society, at which time all the records are reported. She hoped her scheme would work and she would not have to kill anyone.

Every night after she had killed it, the rabbit returned to her. Sometimes she would be at a party, and the rabbit would come and sit close to her, then disappear.

At last the night arrived for the witches' meeting. Everything went well, but just before the assembly was dismissed, the rabbit jumped out of the witch's pot. The old master ordered everybody back to their seats and demanded an explanation. He knew what the witch had done and declared that she would have to die for her disloyalty. Before she could reach home she would die, and she would never find peace, even in her grave. The rabbit would have her blood, and she would have the witch's pot with the rabbit in it.

That night she was found dead on the road.

THE OWL

Near a log house on the bank of the Grand River was a tall pine tree. Night after night an owl hooted and screeched from this tree. At first the people who lived in the log house did not mind the owl. The Natives know the habits of the bird — it travels only at night; but when it keeps going to one particular place, the people begin to get suspicious.

One night a man of German descent visited the people in the log house. They knew him well, for he lived on the opposite side of the river. He had no canoe to get across the river, but when they asked him how he had crossed the river, he laughed. The grandfather of these people said he had known this man for many years. The man knew all about witchcraft, which the white society now calls the lost art.

The people were speaking in their own native language, and the man said he did not understand their language but he understood the

language of the owl who visited them nightly. He told grandfather that the owl which came so often was really a person and that it might be up to some mischief. He told grandfather what to do the next time it came.

That evening the owl was back on the trees again. They threw stones at it but it would not move; it just hooted all the louder. The lady of the house went in and got a gun. She shot at the owl four times but could not hit it. Grandfather got his gun, which his German friend had treated with a witch potion. He shot the owl, and it fell to the ground.

The next day the owl was gone, and that afternoon it was rumoured that an elderly woman had fallen out of a tree. Her leg was broken and she had gone to hospital, where she later died.

It is an old tradition that when a witch in animal form is shot by a treated bullet, a person dies. The owl never returned to that house.

A SUCCESSOR?

About a half-century ago there lived on an Indian settlement a woman who indulged in witchcraft. A few old men and women envied this woman her knowledge and capabilities. She could even turn herself into any bird or animal.

The people on the reservation feared her, and she enjoyed visiting with people she knew did not want to see her. One day she went to the home of a young couple and said she would stay one month. The mother said she was sorry but there was no room for her. Food was put on the table, and the witch was invited to have lunch before she returned home.

The woman told her husband to take the children out of the room and to remain with them while she gave the witch lunch and took her home. When she returned to the kitchen, the old witch was sitting at the table, her long hair falling over her face and her eyes like little holes. The woman went over to her, showing that the hypnosis was having no effect.

The old witch was trembling as she said, 'You are a good investment. You have nerves of iron and I could teach you all my tricks. I shall soon have to pass on my craft to someone like you.' However, there was one condition; the woman would have to take care of her for as long as she lived. The witch's voice was trembling as she told the woman to look out the window and then under the table before giving her a decision.

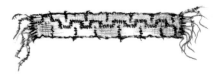

The woman went to the window as directed and then looked under the table. The old witch was gone, but under the table was a fierce-looking animal, with its teeth bared ready to attack her. The woman grabbed her big butcher's knife, kicked the chairs away from the table and said, 'Come out, witch; I just love playing games.' She ran at the dog, but the witch in her own natural voice said, 'Don't kill me. I am not ready to die.'

The woman took the old witch home. When they reached her house, the witch went to unlock the front door. She could not open it and called for the woman to help her. When the woman got to the door and took the key from the witch, she saw that the witch's hand was that of an animal. They unlocked the door, and the witch went into the house. As she stood outside, the woman could hear an animal running around in the house.

A few years later, a message came from the old witch, asking this same woman to come to see her before she died. For two days the woman was undecided, then she got word that the old witch was screaming her name.

She took her young baby and went to see what the witch wanted. As she approached the house, she could hear screams and the witch calling her name. Carrying her baby she walked up to the witch's bedside. The old witch stopped screaming. With wild-looking eyes she caught sight of the baby. 'That's it,' she said. 'The baby will give me peace. The baby will keep the devils away. Oh, please let the baby sit on my breast. She has no sins and I have so many. Please bring her to me.'

The mother put the baby on the witch's breast. A strange calm came over the witch and she went to sleep.

THE BATTLE OF THE WITCHES

A widow of eighty-five lived alone in a small house in the woods, far away from the road. She knew all about bad medicine. In fact, some people called her a witch, saying that they had seen peculiar things at her house.

The old woman liked to visit a young family who lived nearby and who had a small baby. She always picked up the child and danced in a circle, chanting to the beat of a make-believe drum. Suddenly the baby became ill, and the news spread quickly through the community.

A relative of the baby went to visit the child, passing the widow's house on the way. The old woman had brought her wooden churn out on the veranda and was making her dasher go to the rhythm of a tom-tom, while she moved round and round the churn, doing a war dance.

The relative, whose name was Kate, knew the widow was planning some more mischief, and she decided to beat the old witch at her own game. Both of these women knew about medicine. There would be a battle.

Kate did not have any cows to milk nor cream to churn into butter, but she did know magic. She got her old churn from the cellar and, singing the same tune and using the same war cries as the widow, she washed the churn inside and out with her witch's concoction, using the dasher to keep time to her step as she danced around the churn.

Suddenly the dasher began to grow heavier. She stopped and lifted the cover. Her churn was full of choice golden butter; her magic had worked!

The widow-witch was still churning. She was so tired she could not dance any more, so she decided to stop until the next day.

Early the next morning she walked across the field to see the baby and to borrow a small piece of butter for breakfast. She said she had churned all the afternoon before but her cream would not turn into butter. Kate had already warned the baby's mother not to let the widow have any butter, because if she did, the old woman would toss the butter into her churn and it would retract the protective spell Kate had put on the baby. The mother made excuses and refused to let her have any butter.

The widow went home to continue her churning. By nightfall she had still had no success, and she was becoming suspicious.

The next day Kate awoke feeling good about her butter, which she had packed into a large stone crock. But when she uncovered the crock before breakfast, several large frogs jumped out. When she looked carefully inside, she found to her amazement that the crock was full of frogs. The butter had disappeared. Kate was very angry. The widow-witch wanted to play; well, she had found a playmate.

That night, widow-witch was awakened from her sleep by loud talking. She sat up in bed and listened; she could hear her name

being used. She went to the window and listened again. Three men were talking outside. They were making plans to kill her.

She screamed from the open window, calling the baby's mother. The husband heard her screams and hurried over to her house. Widow-witch was hiding upstairs, and when he found her she told him there were three men plotting to kill her.

He persuaded her to return to his house and spend the night with them. On the way to the house, a strange dog approached them and jumped to attack the widow-witch. Before the man could find a weapon, he was startled by the sight of two vicious dogs fighting. Widow-witch had disappeared.

The man left the dog fight and went home. His wife and baby were still asleep, so he went to bed, thinking about the things he had just seen.

No one saw the widow-witch at her house the next day. The man went over to see if anything was wrong. He found her ill in bed and called the country doctor.

The old woman was not well enough to be left alone, so the doctor came to her house and drove her to the hospital. The next day the doctor went to see the neighbour and asked him if he knew how the widow had got all the wounds on her body. They looked like dog bites.

The young man thought that if he told the doctor what he had seen that night, the doctor would not believe him. Looking for some explanation, the man went to the hospital to see the witch. She seemed glad to see him. She told him that each night she dreamed of the past, seeing all the people she had tormented or destroyed. Now her life was over. She had to have her medicine always renewed in order for it to be active at all times, and she said:

'After I was defeated in that fight, all my medicine was defeated too. That is the ruling among the witches.

'I am on my death bed, but I have one last witch's rite to perform. Let me ask you one question: Do you want my home and what goes with it? If you do, it can be my last wish, and what's mine would become yours. Please answer me.'

The man said, 'No, I do not want what is yours. Please do what you like with it.'

The witch died that night, and one hour later her house disappeared completely in flames. When the fire died down, her body turned black like the remnants of her house.

THE WITCH'S POT

It was the beginning of the First World War. Peace was gone from the lives of the Natives, and anxiety and worry affected every home. But every young brave knew in his heart that he must answer the call of duty to his allies who were in trouble. Each one of them had also to fulfil a pledge and renew the treaties of his forefathers.

The Natives who were now in uniform were stationed for training in the capital of their country, the town of Ohsweken.

It was while they were training that strange things began to happen. Every night something visited the barracks, in spite of the guards surrounding the building. It was white and looked like a calf, but when they chased it, it ran like a huge dog. They were forbidden by their officers to shoot at it.

One night the Native soldiers were alerted that something white was behind some trees on the south side of the barracks. They made plans to catch it, and when it came closer, a number of them ran to chase it towards the others, who were waiting. The white calf ran up the hill into the bushes, and when the pursuers got there, all they heard was the cackling of a woman.

That weekend one of the Natives had a leave to visit his home, and as he walked into the house he heard his sister laughing. He recognized the voice as the one he had heard from the white shape in the bushes. Before he could speak she said, 'You should train to run faster.'

He grabbed his old rifle and threatened to kill her, but their mother rushed in just then and demanded to know why he was pointing a gun at his sister. The young man told her and accused his sister of being a witch. The mother told him to sit down and she would tell him the story.

Her husband's mother, she said, had owned the 'Witch's Pot.' Ownership of the pot was hereditary, and it was passed down from one generation to another. Certain conditions had to be met, and if they were neglected, great harm would come to the family.

When the old lady had died, her last request was that the Witch's Pot be given to her granddaughter, the young man's sister. The pot was very powerful, and the girl could change herself into the animal of her choice. She meant no harm; actually, she enjoyed it. Now that his sister had the pot, the mother told the young man, he would bear the responsibility of destroying the whole family if he were to kill the girl.

While his mother was talking, the young man made up his mind that when the time came to go overseas he would never return.

His wish was granted; he was killed in the war.

BOUNTIFUL EARTH

The Natives believe that all things created have a purpose and all creatures should understand and be able to converse with one another.

They understand that the spirit of the wind is just a face with long black hair. It howls as it flies through the air on its own mission, destroying every object in its way. Usually the Natives are warned when there is danger of a windstorm, and they immediately sit on the ground until the storm is over.

It is the belief of the Native people that all things given by the Great Spirit are sacred, even to the food they eat. Corn, beans and squash are called the Three Sisters, for these vegetables were formerly necessary to sustain life.

The Natives understand the voice of the corn and are grateful for its many values. The kernels can be kept for years if stored in a dry place. They do not freeze in the winter, nor do they lose any of their food value.

Many Native families thrive on corn, prepared in many ways. Cornmeal is made out of yellow corn, pounded and sifted into flour. It can be eaten for breakfast with sugar and cream or served as a vegetable with bacon. Corn muffins and cornmeal bread — sometimes called johnny cake — are made from yellow corn.

White corn, lyed and pounded, mixed with water, moulded into thick, round cakes and placed in boiling water until cooked, makes delicious corn soup. This preparation is made in large quantities for national occasions when food is required for many people. Flint corn placed in a pan over a fire makes popcorn for the children.

The husks of corn have many uses. When packed in a bed-sized bag they make a good mattress. They can also be braided and made into floor mats.

OSKENONTON

THE HUNTERS

Two teenage Native boys, who were neighbours, asked their parents if they could go hunting. They had gone many times with their parents in good weather, but now it was in the dead of the winter and the snow was deep. The parents did not want them to go, but finally deciding that they had good training and should be able to take care of themselves, they consented. The boys planned to leave early the next morning.

In the morning, the boys were very careful not to eat a hot breakfast, because they knew the wild game would detect them miles away if they did. For lunch or whenever they got hungry, they carried in their pockets a portion of dried roasted corn, pounded into a fine meal. This would sustain them a whole day. They took their bows and arrows and started out.

On they went, deeper and deeper into the woods. One boy shot a squirrel, which he placed in his hunter's sack. A little farther on, the other boy caught a white rabbit and placed it in his sack. Quite unaware that night was upon them, they suddenly realized that they did not know where they were. They sat down on a big log which was almost buried in the deep snow. They were frightened, for they knew they had lost their way. They tried to call out, but the echo only repeated their calls.

They decided they would stay there until morning — at least they had a place to rest. So they sat close together to keep warm. They were very hungry, for they had eaten up their dried corn, but they still had the squirrel and the rabbit.

They dozed off and slept. After a few hours one boy was suddenly awakened by voices. He called to his friend and told him to listen. They heard the voices again. One voice said, 'These boys are our brothers. If we do not help them, they will freeze. If they would only wake up and let us out.'

The boys jumped down from the log, grabbed their hunting sacks and let the squirrel and the rabbit out. The animals ran as fast as they could into the woods.

The boys got back on top of the log and decided that they could not have heard voices. They had been tricked. They kept on talking in whispers, and soon they were startled by a queer noise. They listened and heard the noise again. It was a tom-tom, and it sounded far, far away. The echo picked up the rhythm until the dense, dark woods were filled with the sound.

The boys jumped down from the log. The sound of the drums sent a fantastic feeling through them, and they began to dance. Round and round the tree they went. The drums became louder and louder.

Out where the moon was shining bright, they could see dozens of men dancing to the tom-tom. The parents of the two boys had formed a searching party for the boys, and the squirrel and the rabbit had shown them the way to find them.

The parents told the boys whenever they entered an unknown wooded area to mark their way well by carving their initials on the trees. Then, if they got turned around, they could follow the marks and would be guided safely home.

49

It was an experience the two boys would never forget, and when the older people talked about the wild animals in the woods, the boys told their people never to kill unless it was for protection or survival.

SPIRIT OF THE RASPBERRY

It is the custom when berries are in season for the Native women to go into the woods to pick the berries to preserve for winter's food.

After rubbing lard on their shoes to keep the snakes away, two women went into the woods in search of berries. On and on they walked. Finally they came to a clearing, and there on the side of a little knoll was a patch of raspberries.

They were very thankful for their rich discovery. They picked all the berries and filled their baskets. When they left to return to their homes, the sun was going down; it would soon be dark.

To their amazement they found that trees and shrubs had closed them in as if they had been there for many years. They did not know what to do, for they could find no way out. It was getting dark, and they were very tired, so they lay down on the soft green grass to rest.

The women wondered if their families would come in search of them. Finally, one of them went to sleep and dreamed that their predicament was the work of some kind of witchcraft. She awoke and told her friend about her dream. They talked in whispers, planning what to do. When morning came they were frightened to see that more trees had grown closer around them. They knew it would be no use to scream.

Then they heard voices saying, 'If you will join with us no harm will come to you.' Remembering the dream that this was the work of witchcraft, they replied that they would not join the voices.

Early next morning they awoke to find a solid wall made out of stones surrounding them. The voices were speaking again, 'There is no escape for you unless you join us. There are only two of us but if you join us you will have the same power and in time control the world.'

They would never give in to the witches. But what could they do?

At that moment they heard a noise like thunder. The ground upon which they stood trembled, and the wall of stone began to crumble to the ground. The trees and shrubs vanished before their eyes. A ball of light appeared, and a dainty little object emerged from it. The rays of the morning light carried a message to the Native women. 'I am the spirit of the raspberry plant. We supply your food from our fruit and medicine from our roots. We have great powers unknown to the world, but when you come to us for sustenance, you come humbly and with prayers. Your reward for your humbleness is our protection. Go now to your homes.'

JIT-GA-RONH-DOH

A long time ago there were no roads through the Mohawk settlement, just a path. When several of the Natives went out together, they walked in a single line, one after another.

Along this pathway there was a huge log, which had been there for centuries. Hunters and other travellers sat on this log to rest and to eat their lunch. It became a landmark for the people, and because this huge log was partly in the water, many other paths led to it from different directions.

The part of the woods where this ancient log lay was like a paradise. Huge archways of climbing ivy decorated the trees, the ground was carpeted with flowers in various colours and all was

protected from the elements by the drooping branches of the weeping willow. One could stay for hours, listening to the songs of the birds flying in and out among the tall trees and watching the squirrels play hide-and-seek with their young.

The birds and the flowers are now gone from this hallowed spot the Natives called 'Jit-Ga-Ronh-Doh.' It is now the great city of Toronto.

One day a hunter of the Mohawk Nation, weary from his long walk in search of wild game for food for his family, sat on the ancient log to rest. Cautiously looking around him, he put his gun down, stretched out on the log and went to sleep.

Suddenly, he was awakened by a thumping sound. He listened; someone was knocking on the door. He realized that there was no door, but the thumping continued. He sat up and looked around and was about to lie down again, when he heard the sound of a bull coming through the trees with all fury. He picked up his gun as the bull came closer. As he aimed to fire, he heard what seemed to him the cry of a newborn baby. Great beads of sweat were upon his brow and he decided to go home.

The next day, two women from the Indian village went into the woods to gather herbs and roots. They had their baskets almost filled when they reached the log and decided to rest before returning home.

Just before they sat on the log, they heard loud cackling laughter. They could see no one, but they did not sit down. They ran through the woods, staggering and panting, and when they reached the village, the inhabitants came running to see what had happened and listened while the two women related their story.

The hunter came forward and related his own experience at the same place the night before.

Volunteers offered to go that night to see what was there. Many suggestions were made: someone might have been killed there ages ago, and the soul of the departed was haunting the place; or perhaps money was buried there, and the owner's spirit was preventing anyone from going near.

At midnight, several hunters prepared their guns. In case this was witchcraft, they imbedded small pieces of silver in each bullet to make sure they hit the target.

They sat upon the log and talked in whispers. It was almost dawn when things began to happen. First they heard a baby crying, then a dog barking and growling. The noises seemed to be coming from underneath where they were sitting, but before they could make a move, a bull was heard charging towards them.

One of the hunters got excited and fired his gun. Something ran out of the log. They shot at it, then chased it. At a distance they could see something lying on the ground.

They had killed a fox. The old chief told them it was the custom of a fox to imitate people and animals. It was only this that had frightened the people so!

POTIONS AND CHARMS

The Natives' remedies have all been given to them by the Great Spirit. The doctors of today cannot use these remedies because they lack faith; their careers are invested in the knowledge of great masters.

The Native uses certain methods to gather his food and medicine. These rituals should not be disturbed, nor should the Natives be drawn away from the faith which guided them so securely before the white man came.

TSIANITO

GAH-NO-DA

One day three Native men were helping their white neighbour to build a barn, when one of the white men fell from the top of the high building. He landed on a pile of stones and was badly hurt.

They placed the injured man carefully upon a plank. The medicine man was notified, and he came quickly, bringing a remedy called Gah-no-da, which heals internal injuries.

This remedy was prepared and administered through faith. The injured man was completely cured in a short time.

HERBAL REMEDY

The Chiefs of the Confederacy were called to another Mohawk settlement to install chiefs to fill in the vacant seats of the departed.

They could not begin the ceremony, since one of the principal chiefs had not arrived. After waiting for an hour, they sent a runner to find out the cause of the delay. The report was that the chief's child, an infant of four months, had cholera. The doctor had given up. The chief would not be able to attend the ceremony.

A Mohawk chief of the Six Nations went over to see the child. He stood by her crib for a moment and then told the anxious mother to have boiling water ready; he would get some medicine.

He walked into their garden, and between the rows of potato plants was the remedy he wanted. It was a sturdy plant, dark green with round, shiny leaves and spread on the ground like ivy.

He went back to the house with the plant, put a portion of it in a cup and steeped it with boiling water. When it had cooled, he gave it to the baby. The child's jaws were set, and he had to force the medicine into her mouth one drop at a time.

The Mohawk chief stayed with the baby, administering the medicine throughout the night. Just before daybreak there was an improvement, and soon the baby was restored to perfect health.

KARAKONHA

During the King's war, the Natives killed many men, but they found favour in one American, whom they did not kill. He was a Negro called Mr Winn, and he lived with the Martin family on the reserve until his death. This gentleman gave a great gift to his friends, the Six Nations, for he discovered while walking through the woods many valuable new remedies, in the form of roots and herbs, for the treatment of different ailments.

A CURE FOR CANCER

One day Mrs Martin developed a lump on her breast. Every day it seemed to grow larger, and she suffered very much. After a lengthy examination, the country doctor said it was a cancer.

Mr Winn had a consultation with the family. He said he could remove the cancer by using a poultice of the cancer root he had seen in the woods. The family agreed that he should try.

Quickly he went into the woods and gathered the medicine. He washed the roots and crushed them, then placed the mixture between two pieces of thin cotton and applied the poultice over the lump. He put a fresh poultice on every day for seven days. At the same time he gave Mrs Martin large doses of blood purifier to expel the poison from her system. This was also from roots and herbs.

At the end of the seventh day, Mr Winn sterilized his pocket knife, gave the patient some brandy and proceeded to take off the poultice. The cancer came with it, except in two places. After giving the woman some more brandy, Mr Winn used his knife to cut everything away. He applied another poultice to heal the wound.

The woman lost her right breast, but she was completely cured and lived to be a very old lady.

THE FORTUNE-TELLER

A maiden and a young Indian brave had been good friends from childhood, and as they grew older, people remarked that they would make an ideal couple.

Finally they announced their engagement. Many of the young people were envious, one especially, whose mother went to extremes to destroy this engagement.

A party was given in honour of the couple's engagement. The woman and her daughter had prepared a love potion, and when refreshments were served, they mixed the love potion in the young brave's food. Almost immediately the engaged man fell for the other woman.

He waited on her, looking adoringly at her face, and never left her side. There was quite a commotion; the people at the party guessed what had happened, because they knew this wicked woman.

The jilted girl could hardly be consoled. Kind neighbours tried to help, but there was nothing they could do. The maiden watched with tears in her eyes as the man she loved with all her heart took the other girl home. He did not even say good-bye. The girl's parents took her home.

Later, a few people called to talk with her parents. They had heard a rumour that the wicked woman was gloating over her success and the extra land she now possessed. Her daughter had the man she wanted, but the best part of all was that the love charm had worked.

These people told the parents about a man from a distant Indian settlement who was able to counteract a love charm. The parents agreed to go to see him. The jilted daughter refused to go with them, saying she wanted to give her thoughts to untangling her life.

These people left for the Indian settlement and located the man, who was also a fortune-teller. He could see what was going on and would help their daughter. He would do more than just counteract the love charm. He would destroy the wicked woman's power, for she had broken many marriages and made many children unhappy.

He used roots to read the girl's fortune, and after going through the usual ritual, he asked the parents to come to the table. He had a concoction in a bowl and took three roots out of his pocket and identified them. The tall one was the man, the fair one was their daughter and the short dark one was the bad woman's daughter.

He placed the three roots in the bowl; the tall root, which represented the man, stayed in one place quivering; then it went round and round in a circle and finally went quickly to the dark root, which was the bad woman's daughter.

The fortune-teller said if they wanted this young man to go back to their daughter it could be arranged. The parents answered that if he would just liberate the young man from the clutches of the wicked woman, they would be happy; they could never enforce the marriage but would let love be the guide. The fortune-teller thereupon destroyed the powers of the wicked woman.

Before the parents arrived home, the spell of the wicked woman had been broken. They found the young man at their home, pleading for forgiveness. After he found out what had happened, he cried in a loud voice, 'Please forgive me. Give me another chance.'

The young girl had made up her mind as to her future, and placing her hand on the young man's shoulder, she said, 'You are free. I have released you, even though I can never forget you. I have made up my mind what to do. Today I shall go into a convent. Perhaps I can forget the humiliation. I will do a little more for you than you did for me: I am saying good-bye.'

The young brave was broken-hearted. The girl of his heart had gone from him. He told her parents he would wait forever. They were indeed sorry about the turn of events, for he was like a son to them.

The girl went into the convent, giving up all worldly activities, and found contentment and happiness. She would not dwell on the thought of what might have been, and the convent life was a hallowed holiness around her.

The wicked woman and her daughter tried again and again to capture the young man — or any man they could work their charms on — but their powers had been destroyed and they could do no more harm.

AN ORPHAN

Daisy was only six years old when she became an orphan. Her parents were killed in a serious accident, and her grandparents took her to live on an Indian reservation. She was very happy and enjoyed listening to the old Indian stories.

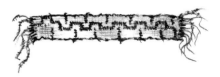

The grandparents' log house was in the woods, and behind it was a stream of spring water. Birds and animals came to drink the fresh, cool water, and Daisy made friends with them.

This stream never froze, and from it her grandfather obtained the Holy Water, which was a cure for all ailments as long as one had faith. He instructed his granddaughter on how to collect the Holy Water. Early Good Friday morning she must rise and give thanks for her night's safety. She must then take a two-quart jar and go to the stream. Facing the rising sun, she must consecrate her soul to an everlasting eternity, beseeching most humbly for the powers of divine healing derived from each drop of the Holy Water. Babies and old people alike had found relief and been cured through the powers of the Holy Water.

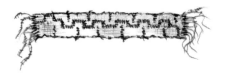

Daisy often wondered about the story of the Hand, which travelled at night and slept during the day. She never wanted to be outside at night, nor would she talk back to her grandparents, for she knew it did not matter where she was — if she was a bad girl the Hand would slap her.

One day she went to her grandfather and told him she did not really believe the story of the Hand. The old man said, 'Come with me,' and they went into the woods.

Grandfather looked everywhere, and Daisy was just going to say, 'I told you I did not believe it,' when they came upon a low-branched chestnut tree. Motioning for Daisy to be quiet, he approached the tree. There was the Hand, asleep on a low branch. She took a good look at it. It was the size of a man's hand, although in colour it was the same as the tree. Grandfather explained that wherever it sat, its colour turned the same as the background. Thus, it is difficult to detect. As soon as night falls, the Hand goes in search of disobedient children.

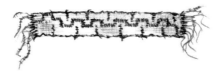

One day while they were walking in the woods, Daisy's grandfather stopped and showed her a path where the witches travelled. When younger, he had watched them many times and would follow them to their witches' palace, where all major decisions were made. At this place of horror, each person appeared according to his witch charm, and his father — Great-grandfather — had even seen the witches in their animal form. The big, fat, slimy serpent was the leader. If any of the witches spoke out of turn, he put them to sleep; and if they did not replenish his witches' pot with human blood, he punished them. The serpent took a survey of all his comrades' activities and told who was lagging behind. The penalty was to give his own life or that of a loved one.

There was no place for tears at this meeting; the serpent was in command. He gave the orders and made all the laws. One could not back out. If anyone made objections the serpent would throw him into a pit of fire. Great-grandfather witnessed many of these meetings. He also learned how to combat the witches' cruel and powerful ways and would not bend to their will. Even the serpent was afraid of a special kind of root which grows in a large, deep swamp. The flower is a beautiful crimson red, and when the plant is pulled out of the ground, the long root will not all come out at once. Grandfather always had this root in his house for protection and a small pine bough over the door to protect his house from witchcraft.

Grandfather told Daisy about one particular incident. His friend had become ill and he went to visit him. There was evidence of witchcraft, so he returned home and made a solution of the red flower root. Going back to his friend, he gave him one-half cup to drink, and the rest he rubbed over his body; and he hung a pine bough over the door. The man soon recovered.

Her grandfather told her that the most important thing in dealing with witches is to be able to protect yourself.

MEDICINE MAN

A medicine man had gathered his medicine and put it into bottles for an emergency. He had a friend who was the doctor in the Native settlement, and he often visited him to discuss certain ailments with him.

The medicine man was out of bottles so he went to see his friend the doctor, who told him to help himself as he had more bottles than he required. The medicine man filled his box with bottles and left the box outside in the shed until the bottles could be washed and filled with his own medicine.

That night the medicine man had a disturbing dream. He saw a woman standing by his bedside, asking him to return her finger. The next night he had the same dream, only this time she was angry. He recognized the woman — she had been dead for three months — and he wondered why she should bother him, since he had had no connection with her.

The next night she appeared to him again, jerked his blankets off and demanded her finger. He got up and went to the shed and brought in the box of bottles, because before he got the bottles he had never had a dream about this woman.

He took the bottles out. One was filled with a liquid, and something was floating around in it. He took the bottle to the light to examine its contents and was surprised to find a part of a woman's finger. As soon as it was daylight, the medicine man went to see the doctor and told him about the disturbing dreams which had caused him to investigate the box of bottles.

The doctor told him he had amputated the woman's finger before she died and had left it in alcohol. He told him to leave it and he would take care of it.

Two nights later the medicine man again dreamed of the woman. This time she said he was causing her a lot of misery. She wanted her finger and she could never rest with the sand around it. He went to see the doctor again and was amazed to learn that the doctor had dug a hole in the ground and thrown the finger into it.

The doctor gave the medicine man the finger, and he buried it in the grave with the dead woman. The woman never returned to haunt the medicine man again.

OSKENONTON

The coming of the white man, or paleface, among the tribal people brought on certain changes in the way the Natives treated their illnesses. The paleface decided that nature caused illness and gave each illness a name the Natives could not pronounce.

The Fortune-teller, the Fairies and the Witches were neglected and forgotten.

A Native who had been a devout member of the Bear Society and who now leaned towards the ways of white society became very ill. He jerked all over, as though he were having a convulsion; his arms and legs became useless, and he was unable to speak. The paleface man called it paralysis. The name of this foreign disease frightened the Native people, but the man's mother was not frightened. She had never lost faith in her tribal beliefs. She consulted a fortune-teller and was told that her son's illness had been brought on through neglect of the Bear Society. The sick man was taken to another Native settlement, and the ceremonial rites of the Bear Society were performed and the Bear feast was held.

The man was released from his chains of torment and became well again.

BREATHING MEDICINE

An eight-year-old girl became very ill. Her parents, sisters and brothers stood around her bed, powerless to help her as she struggled for breath.

They called for a doctor, and when he came he called the family into another room to give each one an injection to prevent the disease from spreading. He called it diphtheria.

An elderly woman offered to treat the child. She used the bark of a plant which has a hole in the centre and grows only in the water. She placed the bark in a container of water and let it boil hard, using the steam to open up the child's breathing. She kept this up for three hours before there was any sign of relief. Then she gave the child catnip tea to promote sleep. She kept the steam in the room for three days, until the little girl became quite well again.

The Native man was ill. A father and the master of the house, he was sorely needed by his wife and three daughters. It was only the beginning of winter, and they prayed that he would not leave them during the season of severe storms. The mother was afraid of the strong winds, but she had much to learn before the winter was over.

The family had called several white doctors, who had given the man pills to kill the pain. One day a neighbour suggested they try Indian medication, since the white doctors had not been successful. But they were modern people; they did not take his advice.

The sick man continued to get worse, and by mid-winter no one came to visit any more. He now needed constant care, and the women moved him to a downstairs bedroom. Two cared for him during the day and two at night. Strange things began to happen in the house they lived in. The doors which led into the sick man's room would not stay closed. But he didn't care — he just lay unconscious in his bed.

One night his wife and a daughter heard the drums of the Natives. The man did not seem to be conscious of the sound, but he became very restless. The drumming continued until two in the morning, then a dog began to howl pitifully underneath his window. This lasted until the break of day. Each night the same thing happened: the sound of the drums and the dog howling.

Again, the neighbour urged the family to consult a medicine man. 'I have good reason to tell you this,' he said.

That night, when the drums started, the sick man became conscious and talked to his wife. He told her that he had been blamed for something he did not do, but he was too weak to tell her any more. That night the mother and daughter went to see a medicine man.

They had not gone far when a round light, about the size of a child's rubber ball, crossed in front of their car lights. It came again and again. Finally they reached the medicine man's house. There was a light at every window, and he said he had been waiting for them. He knew they wanted their fortune read.

They sat near the table with him. The room was dimly lit by a kerosene lamp. Looking into the cup he said, 'When you were on your way here you saw a light go past your car several times. This means that it is too late to help your husband. You have waited too long to come to me. Someone who practises evil medicine has accused him of the unforgiveable act of destroying witchcraft, and the penalty is death.'

The mother and daughter started for home. They were shedding bitter tears and wondering how they could explain to the rest of the family.

When they reached home, the sick man was awake and anxious to know what the medicine man had said. After they told him he said, 'I am being accused of something I did not do.'

He went to sleep. The drums began their nightly ritual. Just before twilight he seemed to be talking to someone. He said the people were trying to cover him up with grass and he recognized one of them. It was his sister-in-law, but she had been dead for many years. The mother and daughters huddled close together and talked in whispers.

The sick man was talking again: 'When a man is dying, take away his pillow if it is filled with feathers, for they once belonged to living things. The pain they bore when they were killed must also be suffered by a dying man.'

The mother wished many times she could do something to comfort her family, but she could only be strong and brave for them.

In the morning the neighbour came again. He was prepared to tell everything he knew. It was worrying him, but at the same time he did not want to cause any trouble.

The sick man was going to die, he said, because a ceremony for his death had been held. Some people, who had accused the innocent man of destroying their witchcraft, had held a ceremony, a dance and a feast. In their midst were a coffin and a doll made out of clay. The doll represented the sick man, and each night the people danced to the drums. They had invited the neighbour to take part in the death dance, and he had done so because everyone who was present at the ceremony had had to participate.

It was the evening of Good Friday when the sick man took his last breath. The neighbour said he had never willed the man to die, even though he had danced in the death ceremony.

THE CYCLE OF LIFE

When there was trouble, the chiefs of the Mohawk Nation often called their people together to renew the traditional rites of their forefathers. The chiefs and the people could not understand death. After they had seen several of their people fall and never get up again, the head men of the Council Fire made certain rules, which was their given right.

They divided the people into clans, then each clan into two divisions. They ruled that when a death occurred in one division, the other would officiate at the funeral. The division that lost one of its members would quietly mourn and say nothing; the other division, who were their cousins, would do the speaking.

The speaker says to the mourners:

'There are many of your own relations still living. There are old folk and children, so let these lift up your minds. Here is the earth upon which we live. Here is water; there are springs and streams of water flowing over the earth. There are plants and trees our Creator has given us. Let these lift up your heart.

'The sky is above our heads. The stars are signs to guide us. The sun gives us light and warmth to make things grow for our food. The moon gives us light; she is our Grandmother. Let these lift up your minds.

'Your grief adds to the sorrows of the dead person. It is not possible to grieve forever. Ten days shall be the time for mourning; after that you must lay your grief aside. When you have lost a loved one, you must bury your grief in their grave; and when the ten days have elapsed, prepare a feast, and the soul of the dead will return and partake of it with you. You can journey with the dead only to the grave.'

When the face of the dead person is unwrapped for his friends to look upon for the last time the speaker says, 'Now let us journey to the grave with the body of the dead. This is as far as we can go, and now we thank all those who have come.' The body is then covered with earth.

The speaker says, 'I have finished speaking for the relatives; now listen to another matter. Let the mourning relatives stop their grieving after the ten days are over. They may then go and do whatever they wish. They are the same as ever and may speak as they please again. They have the right to engage in any national or business affairs; the time of mourning has passed.'

A speaker from the mourning side answers:

'We have heard all that you have said. You have done your part. You must hold in your mind that we thank you for what you have done for us. Now we relieve you of your duties — so it is finished.'

After burial, the dead remain with you in spirit for ten days. During that time it is a tradition that you must remain within the four walls of your home, and on the tenth day you have a condolence ceremony. At this ceremony your tears are wiped away so that you may see and hear again, your parched throat is cleared from the obstacles of sorrow and your ears may hear again and understand the words of wisdom of your ancestors.

The clothes of your departed must be distributed among your friends and neighbours who were kind to you during your bereavement. Nothing must remain in your house.

For the final separation from your departed, you shall prepare your table with delicious food and seat all the guests around the table, leaving a vacant place. One solitary plate must be left in the centre of the table, and a portion of what has been partaken shall be placed in it and left on the table for one night. It must then be taken to the grave of your loved one. When everything is finished and the closing prayers are said, the bereaved are then free to continue living.

If the in-laws of a bereaved widow want her out of their family after the death of her husband (if she has been untrue to him), it is the custom for them to buy her a red cotton dress to wear to her husband's funeral. But if she has been a good wife and they want her to remain in their family, they buy her a black dress for mourning. By this custom, the public knows where the widow stands.

If the widow receives a red cotton dress she does not have to honour the ten-day mourning period. In fact, she can remarry within the ten days.

OHKWAHO

John lived on a reservation. He had been a bachelor for many years. One day John met a girl he liked, and they were married. Although she was from the city she made the best of farm life.

They had not been married long when the woman became very ill. One cold winter night she had to be taken to the hospital. The snow was piled high and the highways were blocked, but with strong determination John cleared a path and got her to the hospital.

The next day he went to visit his wife. The doctors informed him she had an incurable disease and would die before spring. He visited her every day until she died.

John was very sad over his loss and refused to part with any of his dead wife's clothes. He left them hanging in her bedroom, just as she had left them.

The days were hopelessly long and lonely, and John missed his wife very much. He did the farm chores alone, finishing late and going home to eat alone.

On several occasions he thought he got a glimpse of her when he went into the house. Once he thought he saw her go up the stairs. He followed and she went into the room they had shared. He could not find her, but her clothes which were hanging in the room swayed back and forth.

One cold winter night as he sat by the kitchen stove getting warm, he heard a noise on the ceiling. Directly above was a disused pipe hole, and looking up he saw his wife looking down at him. He decided not to go upstairs to bed, but slept instead on chairs in the kitchen. During the night he woke up to find his wife sitting at the table sewing. She looked so real he called out her name. She turned and looked at him, then quickly went upstairs. During that same night he heard singing. It seemed to be coming from the hall. Suddenly the door opened, and eight people came into the kitchen. They walked to the table, sat down and continued singing. They were strangers to him.

The next day John talked with some of the Natives. Two men who understood the ancient traditional beliefs went with him to his home. He took them to his wife's bedroom, where her clothes were hanging neatly and everything was as she had left it. These men told him that he had never really let his wife go to her rest. It was understandable to miss her, but she would never return in human form; and in order to give her peace, he would have to hold a ten-day condolence ceremony and give away all her earthly belongings.

That night John's wife returned to him again. He walked up to her to touch her hand, but she quickly withdrew and disappeared. He made up his mind never to give away her clothes or her belongings. He would be satisfied to live with his wife's ghost.

John lost his desire to continue working the farm and sold all his livestock. He only waited for the night. Neighbours were worried about him and stayed with him as often as they could.

People began to notice that he was losing his will to live and was behaving strangely. One morning they found the poor demented man tying his farm wagon with chains to a post. The health authorities took him away, and shortly afterwards the neighbours heard news of his death.

The two Native men shook their heads and said it was not right to forget one's traditional beliefs.

DEATH IN THE SETTLEMENT

It was in the silence of the night when they were awakened by an unusual sound. The older people in the Mohawk settlement talked in whispers, waiting to hear the noise again. They were concerned, because they had never heard it before.

The young braves were aroused to watch and listen. In those early days, if anything unusual happened which might threaten the people, a runner (or dispatcher) was sent to convey the message throughout all the Native settlements.

While the Mohawks listened, they heard the sound again — the sound of a dog barking.

The old chief of the tribe sent the younger men to find out what the noise was and to report back to him. It was important to know, for it could be a forewarning.

The young men went in a group to investigate. It was difficult to determine whether the sound was being made by a dog or a fox, until the beast stopped right in front of them and howled pitifully. Immediately the young men ran back to tell the old chief that the barking and howling were done by a fox.

The old chief became very sad. There is an ancient tradition that when a fox barks and howls like a dog, it is conveying a message of disaster. The animals and Natives are like brothers: there is a mutual feeling between them, and they understand each other.

The chief sent a runner throughout all the settlements, urging the people to store up food in case of famine and to gather medicine, roots and herbs in large quantities in case of sickness. The roots and herbs would have to be dried, then ground up and placed in containers, with full directions on what each was to be used for.

Within three days, many men, women and children had become ill with cholera. Some of the tribes became almost extinct from this epidemic, but the Mohawks were not as seriously affected. They steeped their cholera remedy — good if the disease was caught in time — and did not lose as many people as their neighbours.

Still, many people died, and the Mohawks buried their dead right where they lay. Because they could no longer have their traditional burial ceremonies, the chiefs of the Mohawk Nation called a meeting. At the emergency Council Fire, the Natives were warned that when someone died they must dig a hole and bury him at once, together with bedding, clothes and everything he had been using.

The old chief then talked about opening up graves. He knew of a small settlement where the Natives had been opening graves and keeping everything they found in them. This settlement had had an

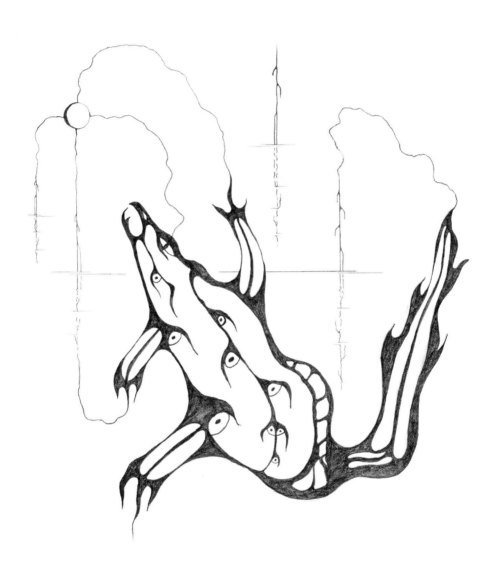

epidemic of smallpox and almost all the people had died. It was the belief of the old chief that they had got the disease from these graves.

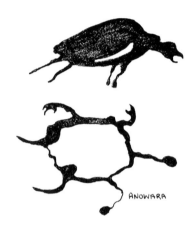

ANOWARA

During a Council Fire the chiefs would remind the people of the obligations of a runner or dispatcher.

When a Native passes away, the runner is given a small bundle of corn kernels. The runner spreads the news of the death throughout the Native settlements, leaving one kernel of corn in each settlement to signify that the message he carries is one of truth sent by someone in authority.

The chiefs said that the dead in their graves know what is going on and know their responsibilities and traditional rights. There is a close tie between the living and the dead. Both are guided by performing certain rituals according to the needs of the living who face earthly trials. Perhaps the dead do not walk in their earthly form, but they still retain the powers given to them from the beginning of time to immortality.

Many years ago the Natives of America would call upon their dead in time of trouble. The call to the dead for help in a national crisis has happened only once on the Six Nations Reserve.

The Natives were threatened with removal from their rich, fertile lands to a place far away, where the waters had been stocked with fish. The white man said, 'You Indians can hunt and fish on this land.'

This, indeed, was a national crisis. The people grouped together hurriedly to summon the aid of their dead brethren. They began their ceremony to counteract the decision beside the grave of Captain Joseph Brant, chief warrior of the Six Nations. On the wooded path to the cemetery, a long table had been laid, covered with Native food prepared in the manner of centuries past.

The ceremony began with a thanksgiving to all things created: to the earth, to the sun, to the moon and the stars. Then came the wailing cry to the dead for help; and the response.

With piercing war cries, the living and the dead danced to the echoing beat of the drums. Round and round the table they went, snatching the food that was placed there for them. The blood-curdling cries of the dead echoed in the night, and their bones rattled as they danced to turn aside the wrongs which were to be committed against their brothers.

Now it happened that a trespasser had invaded the privacy of these ancient rites. No one paid any attention to him and no one told him to leave.

It was almost daylight. Everyone had gone home except the relatives of the young man who had been the trespasser of the night before. They were searching for him, and at midday they found him walking in the woods. But they were not certain he was the same person. This man was only thirty-five years old, yet his hair had turned snow white overnight. His relatives asked him many questions, but he did not remember anything. He did not even know how long he had been walking in the woods.

The people of the Six Nations did not have to move from their homes, because the white people recognized their strength.

A young family had moved from their home on the Six Nations Reserve to live in the city. They had four girls and two boys. The man had found a good job in a foundry, and his wife did day work to help with the expenses. They had left their own home empty, with the windows boarded up.

The house had been empty for about two years when the neighbours got a message to prepare it for the family's return. The man's wife and elder son had died, and his eldest daughter had got married and left home. He had decided to move back to the reserve with the remnants of his family.

When the family moved back home from the city, the father had to leave the children during the day to work for a farmer nearby. He would leave early in the morning and be gone all day. But he was home with his three girls every night.

Mary, the youngest girl, was only four years old, and she missed her mother. In her imagination, she would meet her mother at their home on the reserve and she would give her mother a small bundle containing a cracked cup, a pair of old stockings, a piece of faded ribbon and a page out of an old magazine. Mary had a crude little bundle like this and carried it with her everywhere she went.

The older girls began to abuse and neglect their little sister during the day. With her bundle held tightly in her hand, Mary would wander to a nearby house. This neighbour had an eight-month-old baby, and Mary liked to play with it. The neighbour was kind to Mary and gave her a cookie and a glass of milk when the baby was fed. In the evening Mary would return home in time to meet her father, who was pleased that his little daughter had found a friend.

One day the two older sisters locked the doors and would not let Mary out to go play with her little friend. She cried all day, and by evening she was lying still on her bed. They tried to arouse her by saying they had unlocked the door and she could go and play with the baby, but there was no response. Their father returned and found Mary unconscious. She had a high temperature, but she still held on tightly to the little bundle which was for her mother.

The father went across the road to talk to the neighbour, who told him she had heard Mary's screams but had not seen her the whole day. The father felt very sad, remembering his wife, who had loved their family and done her best for them right up to her last day.

The neighbour agreed to drive a horse and buggy to take Mary to see a white doctor in the city. They left early the next morning. Mary was so happy to see the little baby that she held her tight all the way to the city. The doctor took Mary into his examination room. A little while later he called the neighbour in and explained that Mary had an incurable fever and that she would die very soon, in spite of all the care he could give her.

The doctor was right. In a few weeks Mary did die, holding her little bundle to take to her mother.

The family was very sad. The father had only two girls left. His son had found a good place to work and would not be returning home. The two daughters were now teenagers, and their only interests were to be with the rough crowd in the neighbourhood, breaking all the traditions and rules of their forefathers.

Their father tried to reason with them, saying he did not mind if they went out with the young people, but he wanted them home every night at a respectable time. The girls agreed, but they made up a plan to fool their father. As soon as night came and everybody had gone to bed, they would creep downstairs to meet their friends and go to parties where firewater flowed freely.

One night when they stepped out of the house, they saw something white in front of them. They looked more closely and saw that it was their mother. The beaded buckskin garment she had worn in her coffin had become snow white. She was a beautiful woman, and stood there with a lovely smile on her face.

The girls ran back into the house and crept up the stairs and into bed without disturbing their father.

The next time they tried to get away, their mother was waiting for them again. The third time, when they ran into the house and up the stairs, their mother was right behind them.

They screamed for their father. He jumped out of bed and rushed to their room.

As the three huddled together, they could hear someone moving around downstairs. There was a noise as though the cookstove was being used and the sound of dishes being placed on the table. The father and daughters became frightened and screamed until their neighbour heard them. She lit a kerosene lantern and walked across the fields to their house.

As she entered the kitchen, she saw something on the table. When she examined it, she saw that it was the little bundle which contained a cracked cup, a pair of old stockings, a piece of faded ribbon and a page out of an old magazine. The bundle had been placed beside Mary in her coffin, but now it was there on the kitchen table.

THE VACANT LOT

Two business partners, a Native and a non-Indian, had had a prosperous business in another country and had sold it at a great profit. Looking for a good location on which to build a new business, they chose a vacant lot next to the boundary line of an Indian settlement.

People in the neighbourhood of the vacant lot had seen many mysterious things happen there, and many were afraid to pass or walk near the place at night. Sometimes they saw a light bobbing up and down. Once a man who was under the influence of firewater spent the night there. In his state of mind he didn't care for anything, but during the night he heard unnatural sounds and was suddenly lifted high off the ground and thrown onto the highway that went past the vacant lot. He told the people who found him about the frightful things he had seen and heard, but they did not believe him.

One day the two businessmen had the lumber and materials for their new building delivered to the lot. But next morning when the workmen arrived to begin construction, they were amazed to find all the material scattered on the highway.

An aged man from the Indian settlement nearby told the businessmen what to do. They listened, but when he finished talking, they sneered and laughed at him. They told him that if he could solve the mystery of the vacant lot, they would give him the land and all the building material; if he could not, he would have to work for them for five years without any wages, only his board and lodging. They all agreed to this bargain, and one of them wrote it down on paper and the three of them signed.

That night the Native went to the cemetery and got grave dirt and went to the vacant lot. The night was dark; he built a small fire and went through a traditional ceremony, pleading to the dead whose dust he had in his hand to reveal to him the mysteries of the vacant lot.

He lay down on the ground with the grave dirt in his hand and went to sleep. He dreamed that someone was waking him up, and a voice said, 'Get up and look. Tell me what you see.'

The Native got up and looked. Two men with their hats pulled low over their eyes were beating a man whose features he could not make out because there was so much blood covering his face. Then the apparition was gone and the Native lay down and went back to sleep. Just before daylight he heard the voice again. 'Get up and look. Your fortune depends on what you see.'

The Native got up again. The two ruffians he had seen before were gone. The man who had been so viciously attacked was coming towards him with arms outstretched. He sat down beside the Native and told him he was a brave man to be there. Because of his bravery, he would tell him everything about the vacant lot.

The murdered man's parents, he said, had been very wealthy and had had a business on this land. He was their only son. The two masked men were the men who had just bought the vacant lot. They were greedy for money and had robbed and murdered his parents many years ago. Before they were killed, however, the parents had turned all their riches over to their son, who had put the money into a strongbox and buried it.

After the parents were dead, the two men returned and demanded the hidden wealth from the son. When he refused, they killed him. Since his death, the murdered son had been haunting the vacant lot, trying to keep people away, while waiting and hoping that someone who deserved the money would come to the lot. The murdered man had chosen the Native.

The Native went back to sleep after his conversation with the murdered man. At daybreak the two killers returned to the vacant lot to find the old man and his friends who had witnessed the bargain waiting for them.

The two killers demanded an explanation for the strange happenings on their land, and the Native in turn demanded that an officer of the law be present when he gave them their answer.

The officer arrived, and the old man narrated his experience of the night before. The two businessmen told the officer that this story was not true, and since the old man had not solved the mystery of the vacant lot, they would take him and he would be their slave for five years.

The Native then announced that he was ready to produce the evidence, and while they watched, he dug a hole in the vacant lot and located the body of the murdered son.

The businessmen were arrested, and the Native became the owner of the vacant lot and its buried treasure.

DYAUNHRONHKO

When a Native baby is born, the midwife, who is also a Native, follows the traditions of her ancestors. The new baby is given the medicine of roots and herbs to purify its system and control convulsions, one of the most dreaded children's afflictions. After the baby takes this purification treatment, and before any nourishment, it receives a spinal treatment. The midwife then treats the baby's throat so that it may never be subject to choking.

The midwife also takes care of the mother. The mother must start the baby by feeding it her own milk, as it contains all that is required to give the baby a good start for a long, healthy life.

THE NATIVE BABIES

Two people living on a Native settlement had suffered much sorrow and heartache, as all three of their children had died at three months of age.

Baby Carol, the first child, could never be left alone in a room. At night she would sleep only with the light on and would wake the minute it was turned off.

One day the mother went outside to get a pail of water from the hand pump. Hearing the baby scream, she left her pail and ran back into the house. The baby was in her crib, her eyes staring at something. The mother took her out and tried every way to arouse her but failed. The child died the next day.

In time, she had another baby and named her Lynda. She was healthy and her mother loved her and hoped she would be all right.

After giving baby Lynda her lunch, she put her to bed for her nap and went outside to hang the blankets she had washed. Suddenly she heard loud screams from her baby. Terror filled her heart as she ran into the house. There was her baby, staring up at the ceiling, gasping for breath. She picked her up and ran outside screaming, hoping someone would hear her. A neighbour came and the doctor was called. He did his best, but like the previous baby, this child died at three months of age.

Viola, the third child, was her father's pet. He told his wife that nothing must happen to this child. They never left her alone, and when she was nearing three months, they took special care.

The parents had gone to bed one night when suddenly the familiar loud scream awakened them. It was a repetition of the previous behaviour. This child too had dilated and staring eyes. At the age of three months, their third child died.

This couple had deserted their Native faith and gone into white society. They had forgotten the old traditions and legends. Their neighbours, who were of the original faith, wondered how long it would be before this couple realized their mistake in trying to join white man's society.

Two Native women who had great compassion for this couple decided it was their right to talk to them. They were graciously received and the couple listened very closely to what these women told them.

The two Native women explained that sometimes a very high price must be paid when the teachings of the ancestors are disregarded. They advised that if the couple were to be blessed with another child they must remember to follow the customs of their people.

THE WHITE MAN COMES

In the early days, Natives often saw visions or apparitions which they knew had special meaning or were forewarnings.

The Chiefs of the Six Nations Confederacy were warned through visions and dreams before the coming of the white man.

A LOOK INTO THE FUTURE

In his dream, the old chief saw his pony with two heads. One head was Native with head-dress, and one was blond. The blond strangled the Native head after he had gained his purpose.

In another dream, the old chief was walking on a narrow path beside a snake rail fence. After he had walked a long distance, he came to a section where someone had left a trail of Native skulls hanging on the fence as if on exhibition. The old chief stopped, but one of the skulls urged him to move on. In the distance he could see a commotion, and as he drew near he could see people fighting. Nearby was a large chasm, and in the bottom was a sailboat. As the people fought, all the blond heads were thrown into this chasm. Some of them landed in the sailboat, others were lost.

The old chief remembered the voice of the wind, 'I will destroy and take away that which torments my people.'

Deh-ha-ronh-ya-ga-nel-reh (He-sees-the-skies) is a brother of the Little People. His mission is to travel where the Onh-gwe-honh-weh (Natives) live, but he only becomes visible when his people are in danger.

Shortly after the coming of the white man, Deh-ha-ronh-ya-ga-nel-reh reported to the Native people what he had seen across the great waters; people who had been dead for centuries walked the streets of the foreign cities. He had also seen huge gatherings of people conspiring to destroy one another. They had no thought for peace and were making weapons by night and day to destroy lives and gain power.

Deh-ha-ronh-ya-ga-nel-reh told the Onh-gwe-honh-weh to hold fast to his faith and to spread the message of the Tree of Peace, which means peace and goodwill to all mankind.

Deh-ha-ronh-ya-ga-nel-reh said to the Mohawk Nation, 'Now that I have reminded you of the laws of the Tree of Peace, I shall bid you farewell in words of both warning and hope. If men should ever become indifferent to the Confederacy, I may stand here again among your descendants. If the Great Peace should fall, call on my name in the bushes and I will return.'

THE BUNDLE OF FIVE THINGS

A man of Native origin had disregarded the teachings of his fore-fathers and taken up the ways of the new white culture. One day as he was sitting by the river, an island appeared in the water. On the island stood a beautiful castle of gold.

A voice came from the golden castle: 'Across the river toward the sunset is another world. People live there whom you have never

seen. These people are good, they have no evil habits and they are honest. I shall give you a great reward if you will take the five things in this bundle to these people.'

The bundle of five things contained a flask of rum, a pack of playing cards, a handful of coins, a violin and a decayed leg bone. Immediately the Native prepared to explore this new world. He took many bundles of the five things and divided them among the Natives of the great earth island.

The voice from the gold castle laughed and said, 'These cards will make them gamble away their wealth and idle their time; this money will make them dishonest and they will forget their old laws; this fiddle will make them dance with their arms around women other than their wives; this rum will turn their minds to foolishness and they will trade their world for more of it.'

It was a sad fate for the man of Native origin. He had a wife and two boys, and they had moved from their native home to live in the city. It had become a habit for him to go out every night with his city friends to a nearby saloon. His wife became ill from worry, and the boys were old enough to share their mother's worries.

The husband agreed to build a house on their own home land, and they were all very happy there until he started going back to his old haunts. He would often come home in a dangerous mood. Once he attacked the mother.

When the man came home from the city on weekends, the mother and the boys would hide in the swamp until he went to sleep. Each week, he checked the boys' school work. If their report cards were not satisfactory, he took the boys down into the basement and gave them a sound beating.

It was near the end of a school term, and report cards would soon be sent out. The younger of the two boys had scored a poor rating in his school work, and he was very frightened of his father. He would not eat and stayed by himself in his room, knowing too well what was waiting for him.

One day, after they had had their evening meal, the boy went back to his room. The father had not yet returned from the city. When he returned in his usual stupor, he demanded that they all sit down to eat their dinner. The mother and her son knew it would not be wise to cross his will, so they prepared the table. The man yelled for his younger son and wanted to know where he was. The mother answered that he was in his room doing his school work.

The man said, 'When I get home I want my family to be here. You call the boy. When he comes down, I shall teach him how to respect his father.' The older boy ran up the stairs calling his brother's name, but there was no answer. The boy was not in his room, and the father was very angry.

They looked for the boy, and the father went dashing down to the basement. Suddenly there was silence, and the mother and her son ran down to see what had happened. There was the husband staring at a body hanging from a rafter, a report card in its hand. The body was that of his own son, cold in death.

It was a cruel awakening for this man. He could not be consoled. His friends at the saloon collected money for him, but when he received the money he would not keep it.

Every night his wife found him in the basement, looking up at the beam from which the boy had been hanging, repeating, 'Why do you not come down, son? Do not be afraid.'

The man found no comfort in that house. After a lapse of time, he sold it and built a new one, miles away from where the tragedy had happened, but that was not the answer. He stopped drinking, but he could still see his son hanging from the beam with his report card in his hand.

Native people had a way of travelling without being seen or heard, so when people saw the empty canoe they thought nothing about it. There was an emblem on the canoe, the picture of a turtle, indicating that the owner was a Mohawk.

One moonlight night, people who lived in the village of the white man saw the canoe with six Natives in it. They were from different Nations, and each wore a head-dress according to his tribe. As they glided past, the villagers could hear them chanting to their drums.

The people were still on the bank of the river when the canoe came back. It was empty except for a little white rabbit, who sat majestically in the centre holding his paddle. The village people began to ask one another, 'What does this mean?'

When an old man in the village heard what the people had seen, he told them what had happened when he was just a little boy. Natives had once owned and lived in the village. One night they were cruelly attacked by a large white army. Everybody was killed except one Native, and the Little People changed him into a white rabbit.

This white rabbit could cause destruction or death, but if he found favour in someone, he could do much good. When this white rabbit is seen by people, something is going to happen. It is no use to shoot at him, because he is indestructible. Now that the villagers had seen the white rabbit, anything might happen. He could be out to avenge his people.

A six-year-old boy had been a helpless cripple all his life. He was left on the bank by his widowed mother, who was a Native, while she walked to the village for food. As he sat by the river watching the water, a canoe glided towards him. It seemed to be empty, but when it stopped in front of him, a white rabbit jumped out and sat down beside him.

The boy said, 'Hello, white rabbit. I wish I could run and jump like you.' The rabbit asked him if that was all he wished for, and

the boy said, 'That is all. Then I could help my mother, who works so hard.'

The white rabbit jumped up and told the crippled boy that from then on he would be able to run like a rabbit. The rabbit turned some cartwheels and cried, 'Come on, you're not going to let your mother carry the groceries home.'

The little boy jumped up and found that he was not a cripple any more. He ran all the way to the village, right into the grocery store where his mother was doing her shopping, calling, 'Mother, I can walk — the white rabbit made me walk — I can run fast like him!'

The news spread that the crippled boy could walk, and crowds flocked to the village store, asking hundreds of questions. To them, the boy did not make much sense. He said a white rabbit had made him well.

The old man heard the story of the crippled boy and he went to the store. People made room for him to pass and he walked over to stand beside the boy. He told again about the slaughter of the Native people who had once owned the village and how everyone had been killed but one man.

'The Little People loved the Natives of this village,' he said, 'and they saved this man by turning him into a white rabbit. It is the nature of the Natives to love little children, and that is why the white rabbit had compassion for the crippled boy.'

After the boy had listened to the old man's story, he cried to the villagers to give back to the Natives that which was rightfully theirs. No one spoke.

The old man continued: 'It has been said that the empty canoe and the white rabbit are out to avenge the Natives.'

Then the people gathered around the boy, giving him messages for the rabbit and buying groceries for the boy and his mother. Finally the boy told them to stop. He said, 'I have been helpless all these years. Sometimes my mother and I have been very hungry, but no one cared. Now, when you think you can profit by it, you do things for us, thinking the white rabbit will do something for you.

But I have a message for you. The white rabbit said that no one can buy happiness — it can only come from a pure heart.'

MUSEUM

The non-Native curator of a museum liked her work very much.

In this museum was everything the Iroquois people had used in their daily routine of living: the crude utensils and the pottery, the hollowed-out log where they did the corn pounding and the big black iron pot used to cook the meat or to make corn soup for national conventions.

The battle axe, tomahawk, scalping knife, bow and arrow and ancient guns which were used at the time of the American Revolution were there, along with the powder pouches in which the ammunition had been kept and the old rocking chair where the master of the house had reclined after a long day's trudging through the woods. Beside the chair lay the moccasins he wore, the soles of which were dark and shining from the constant wear of many moons. Nearby lay his pipe of peace, together with a bowl of the sacred tobacco into which he had dipped his pipe many times. The Native was a good man, slow to anger. But when aroused to trouble or danger, he would quickly become a vicious wolf seeking revenge.

The second floor of the museum was filled with happy memories; a crib in which many babies had slept stood in one corner, and there were old beds with corn-husk-filled mattresses. Even the creaking floors could not disturb this tranquil room.

In the next room, faces were hung on all four walls. Masks held special meaning for the Native people, the medicine mask which could cure diseases and the mask which drove away the evil spirit.

97

Each face is alive and constantly on the alert, watching the curator. She is not an Indian and is not aware of the needs of the masks.

One day the curator became very ill. Her doctor gave her medicine, but after two weeks she was much worse and had lost four pounds.

An old chief went into the museum and noticed how ill she looked. She told him she could not eat and the doctor did not know what was wrong with her.

The old chief told her that the centuries-old treasures — especially the masks — required attention. He also told her that the Natives honoured these treasures and if anyone neglected these possessions he would soon become ill. He told her what to do and that if she obeyed his instructions she would soon be well again.

The curator was to have a dead feast for everything in the museum. The Native people were to prepare the food, including a special false-face feast for the masks. Small bundles of the sacred tobacco must be hung behind each mask.

All these things were accomplished, and the curator became well and strong again.

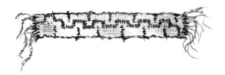

Not far from the museum was an antique shop. Some dealers had gone through the reservation and bought a quantity of false-face masks, bows and arrows and Indian dolls, as well as a large iron pot and a mug in the form of an Indian head.

Now it happens that when a Native of a tribe makes anything, he includes his personality and traditional beliefs, and when the article is completed he talks to it as if it were a human being. If it is a bow and arrow, it must be accurate in what it is destined to do. If it is a mask, it, like a person, demands to be fed; if it is not fed it can be treacherous. The Indian dolls have their own ways. The large iron kettle has a history of centuries past: Hiawatha saw his sinful ways in the reflections of the kettle; human beings have boiled in the same kettle and could do so again. The proud Indian's personality is entombed in the Indian Head mug. The other objects follow his advice because he has the head of wisdom.

Nothing happened the first night at the antique shop, only strange noises the people had never heard before. They could hear people talking, but no one was there.

The next morning they heard noises again: someone was moving around in their shop. Upon investigation they found that everything was where it had been placed.

At nightfall the people were a little nervous, but nothing happened until the next night. It was dark and windy, and the rain came down in torrents. As they listened they could hear loud screams. People began to talk in a language they could not understand, and there was another loud scream and a crash. The people waited for daylight before they went down into the shop. There was the granny mug on the floor, broken in small pieces. The Indian mug sat up on the shelf as if to say 'I did that.'

The following night there was another commotion. When they entered the shop the next morning they found that an arrow had pierced the heart of an American statue. All the ancient wax dolls were scalped and thrown into the large black pot. The false-face masks were scattered all over the floor.

It could be plainly understood that the ancient objects of the Natives were out of place with their white neighbours.

CHANGING RITES

There occurred a division in religious beliefs among the Natives. The newcomers from the Old World had built a Christian church on their lands, and they had talked to the Natives, encouraging them at first not to change or stray from the belief of their ancestors in the Great Spirit, the Creator of all things, who brought peace and love to all mankind.

A NEW RELIGION

The wailing of the four winds around the church steeple could be heard for many miles; the dark clouds moved in rhythm, and at the stroke of midnight, the graves in the cemetery opened up and the sleeping dead arose from their slumber and marched into the church.

A Native businessman was troubled about this new religion. He was walking home from a tavern after an evening of drinking with his friends when he heard the church bells. Stopping near the church, he saw the procession of the dead into the church. Then he heard a whisper in the wind, urging him to go home.

He had never been inside the church, but something seemed to urge him to go. He followed the procession and walked in behind them.

The old organ was playing the hymns of long ago. Everybody stood up to sing, so he sang too. He felt very good being there. It was dark in the church, and his feet were cold and clammy, but everyone kept on singing amid the sound of the wailing wind.

Suddenly the man felt very tired and he sat down and went to sleep. The next thing he knew, someone was shaking him to wake

him up and saying, 'Get up now before someone sees us.' He did not know how long he had slept.

When the ghostly group went outside, the four winds were still howling around the church steeple, bending the trees almost to the ground. The winds seemed to be angry, for it was almost daylight and the bodies from the grave had overstayed their time. They began to run.

The whisper of the wind came again. 'Run fast, you are one of them.' The businessman ran behind them into the cemetery and fell headfirst into an open grave. He did not know he was in the grave. He was so tired he lay down and went to sleep.

At his home there was excitement, concern and worry. The master of the house had not returned home. Police and kind neighbours searched everywhere for him. The proprietor of the tavern told the police the man had left there at midnight. The search continued all day, and then it was night again.

The wailing of the wind awakened the man in the grave. He tried to get out but the grave was too deep. The four winds whispered, 'Be quiet, you are now one of them.' The man began to scream in terror, and a passerby heard him and notified police.

The police took lanterns into the cemetery and found the man in the open grave. When they helped him out he had in his hand a piece of cloth covered with mould.

The Native knew his horrible experience had been the result of straying from his own faith. He was depressed, and all he could hear was the whispering of the four winds, 'You are now one of them.'

BETTY AND HER FRIENDS

Betty was a frail little girl who lived on an Indian settlement. She was not very happy. Her parents indulged in the white man's fire-

104

water, and she was sadly neglected. At night she was alone and often cried herself to sleep.

She had two dear friends, a boy her own age, named Jimmy, and a large black collie dog. The boy knew how unhappy she was and he wished he could help her. In the evening he would tell her the stories his old grandparents had told him about the heaven world and the different signs in the sky.

Betty was eager to learn about heaven and the life hereafter. In time, she learned not to mind all the trouble her parents created. There was no room for ugliness or unhappiness in her heart. She was preparing herself for the time when she would never be hungry or cold again.

Her friend told her about the stars. Every time a star falls it is a sign that someone has gone to heaven, and every time a star is close to the moon a little child will die. She was not afraid of death, because her friend had told her about the angels playing their golden harps on the beautiful stairway which led to heaven.

One day the little boy did not come to visit the girl, and even black collie stayed away. She was very lonely and she watched for him all day, but he did not come.

That evening as she sat alone by the window watching the stars and the moon up in the heavens glowing silver in the black sky, she saw a star fall. Betty clapped her hands with delight. She knew someone had gone to heaven, and she knelt by her bed and said her prayers.

Early the next morning the boy's father came to see Betty. She was very happy to see him, and he did not know how to break the news to her. At last he sat down beside her and told her that his son had gone to heaven to stay with the angels.

The little girl smiled softly and said, 'I am so happy he is with the angels. He wanted to be there. Now I will never be alone; I can see him every day.'

When Betty saw the boy in his casket, she stared for a second, then kissed him and whispered, 'Please tell the angels how lonely I am and to take me also. You have been my only friend.'

She told his parents that she had known someone had gone to heaven, because she had been at the window and had seen the star fall. They buried the boy where Betty could see the grave from her window. Black collie never left her side.

One night she had a dream and began screaming. Her mother came into her room to find her sitting up in bed, both arms outstretched and crying, 'Jimmy, please take me and black collie, please.'

When her mother asked her what was wrong, she replied, 'Oh, Mother, you would never understand. Jimmy is up there on the golden stair, beckoning to me to come, but I cannot go unless black collie can go too. Mother, I wish you could come too, but I don't think you can.' Pointing to the skies she said, 'There he is again on the golden stair, and black collie is there too.'

That night Betty died in her sleep. No one was there with her, but her prayers were answered. Before her own funeral was over, black collie was hit by a car and died.

Jimmy's parents were not too unhappy. Their son had been ready to accept death, and through his teaching Betty had longed to go in search of love and happiness. Now there were three graves: for Jimmy, Betty and black collie.

TSIANITO

The ancient folkways of the people were almost destroyed when a new system was introduced, based upon the framework of the old. The societies and orders that upheld the older religious rites were discredited by a prophet claiming a revelation from the Creator. The new religion of the Six Nations was the code of a Native called Handsome Lake.

The rites of the different societies were held in secret places after the advent of the prophet Handsome Lake, and with the acceptance of his new religion by the majority of the Natives, the older or original beliefs were blended into the new one. Some of the Natives call the original belief their Old Testament.

Each society has a legend that portrays the founder as a lost hunter, an orphan or a restless youth, curious to know what is in the great beyond. Most of these adventurous people had great difficulties, and they sometimes had dreams about strange animals who took part in their ancient rites and then sent them back to their own people to teach them the secrets of their encounters. These secrets were preserved in each case by the society to which the restless youth belonged.

There are many different Indian societies. One group is dedicated to the Little People, who have been known to cure certain ailments. This society has ceremonial rites which contain one hundred and two songs, divided into four groups. The first has fifteen songs, the next twenty-three, the third, thirty and the fourth, thirty-four songs. During a ceremony, all these are sung in darkness. It is the belief that the spirit members of the society join in the singing. People in attendance detect their voices during the ceremony. The drum and the horn rattle are used to keep time during a brief dance.

The rites of the Little People have the power to grant wishes or change a person to a supernatural being. Sometimes the ceremonies are performed to quiet the spirit of the society.

Meetings of the societies or religions may be called in case of illness. Sometimes a patient is haunted or troubled by certain sights or sounds, and the rituals can be invoked against these.

In some societies, medicine charms are always in demand. Most of these involve magic animals like the horned serpent, the blue panther, the white beaver, the corn bug and the naked bear; others are the Naked Leg, the Hand and the Wind Spirit.

If neglected, some of these charms can bring harm to the owner, and their evil influence can be warded off only by the ceremonies of the charm involved. These ceremonies have been known to help many people who have been afflicted. They are not the same as the practices of the medicine men, who treat sick people with herbs, roots, plants and the bark of trees.

The Society of Otters is a band of women who propitiate the Otters and other water animals. These exercise an influence over the health, fortunes and destinies of men. The Otter, which is the chief of the small water animals, including the fish, is a powerful medicine animal.

The Society of the Otters has no songs and no dances. Its members organize to give thanks to the water animals and to retain their favour. When one is ungrateful, like a wasteful fisherman or a hunter who kills muskrats or beaver without offering the sacred tobacco to their spirits, he becomes ill. The members of the society go to a spring and conduct a ceremony, after which they go to the sick man and sprinkle him with spring water, which makes him well again.

THE OLD BROWN HOUSE

The old brown house, which had stood on the banks of the Grand River for many years in solemn solitude, now had lights glaring from every window and people going in and out.

An old woman lived there with her only son. She was very ill and near death. Kind neighbours had heard about her illness and had stayed all night to help in any way they could. The sick woman was talking. The neighbours drew near to listen to her. She told them there were little children pulling at her bed-clothes and at her arms, and even at that moment, they were crawling on her bed, whispering that she must go away with them. There were other little people, carrying bowls of steaming hot food. Still others followed with tiny golden harps, playing beautiful strains of heavenly music.

A strange calm came over her face. The neighbours were frightened that this might be the end. They called her son, and he came and stood at her bedside. She opened her eyes and said: 'Son, you know who these Little People are, but you do not want them in our house.' The neighbours questioned him. He said he had forsaken the ancient ways and did not believe in the Little People.

The sick woman was talking again, and they hastened to her bed-side. This is her story.

When she was a little girl, the Little People saved her from drowning, and that same afternoon her own mother held a thanksgiving ceremony for them, repeating the ceremony every year afterwards. Now, because of her son's objections, the woman no longer held a thanksgiving ceremony. Thus, she now had to go away with the Little People.

Her son ran to her bedside. Putting his arms around her, with tears streaming down his cheeks, he said, 'Mother, I am so wrong. Let us have the thanksgiving ceremony at once, if the kind neighbours will help.'

A long table was put up, and the people who were members of the Little People Society brought the required things for the occasion — plenty of food and pieces of silk material to replenish the Little People's wardrobe. The chosen speaker conducted the ceremony, first placing the sacred tobacco upon the dying embers of the fire and then most solemnly pleading for the return of this woman's health.

After the ceremony, the singers of fairy songs came forward to finish. They sang their songs and marched to the beat of the water drums. In the early hours they partook of the sacred food and later went chanting into the woods and scattered the pieces of silk material.

The sick woman arose from her bed and lived to a ripe old age, together with her son, in their little brown house.

ON THE GRAND RIVER

It was after the invasion of the white population that the Little People took refuge in out-of-the-way places, but they did not lose their powers. They left the old settlements and went into the crevices of rocks, but if you called to them on a clear, quiet night, they would answer. They had to hide because times had changed and witchcraft had become evil and dangerous and was being used to destroy many lives. Greed had entered the Native settlements, destroying purity, honesty and love.

Finally, the white man's wars reached the settlements. Firewater flowed freely, like the rivers which now divided the Native lands from those of the paleface. The Little People watched these events with sadness.

TSIANITO

THE LITTLE PEOPLE AND JOSEPH BRANT

The Little People had come to a decision. They would watch and wait for an honest Native who would be deserving to wear the

Magic Moccasins and to guide, lead and preserve the rights of the original people (Onh-gwe-honh-weh).

One day they found their brave. He was to save his people from utter destruction.

Early one morning this young brave arose from his bed. He had had a dream in which he had been rewarded with Magic Moccasins, on the condition that he would help his people. In the dream, he had placed them upon his feet; and now, as he stood by his bed, he looked down at his feet, and there were the Magic Moccasins. He went to the window and, facing the sun, he vowed he would help his people, the Six Nations, and die if need be.

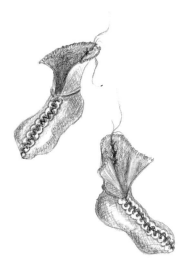

This young Indian brave was no other than Captain Joseph Brant, who was to serve his people so well that no white man's law has been able to completely destroy the independence of the Six Nations people upon the land where they now reside.

The Six Nations conquered much of what is now Canada before the British laid claim to the area. The entire colonial history of Canada is interwoven with the story of the Six Nations. They are the makers of history, and the names 'Ontario' and 'Canada' come from their language.

Joseph Brant, guided by the Magic Moccasins, was involved from the age of thirteen in the exploits of the Six Nations tribes. The whole course of his life showed that he was the most remarkable Indian of his time. During the American Wars, it was the intellectual power of Captain Brant that held the vast majority of the Six Nations people loyal to the British cause.

After the American Wars came to an end, the Natives of the Six Nations lost their homes in the United States and had many problems to contend with. First of all, they had to prove to the King that they had fought for his cause before they could be recompensed for their losses. They had preserved all the scalps of the King's enemies whom they had killed, and the King was satisfied and gave them a grant of land along the Grand River in Ontario.

In times to come, the nations of the world will see and hear again the continued activities of the Magic Moccasins.

Shortly after the coming of the white man to the interior of America, a trading post was established on Burlington Bay, where Dundurn Castle stands today.

Over the years many people came to this post. One day a man by the name of Campbell came into the post and asked the trader to take him to the Mohawk village to see Joseph Brant. The trader hitched up his sleigh, and during the long drive, he told Mr Campbell about the Brant family.

At that time Joseph Brant was the speaker for the Six Nations people, and he often went to Philadelphia to meet with the members of the Congress of the United States.

Mrs Brant dressed in the Indian fashion, her large black eyes in harmony with her expressive features. Her blanket was usually made of silk and the finest English cloth, bordered with a narrow strip of embroidery. Her jacket and petticoat were always of the same material, with leggins of scarlet colour, fitted to show her well-shaped limbs. Her moccasins were beautifully decorated with beads. Mr Campbell continued his description of Catherine Brant:

'She is five feet, ten inches in height and as straight as the cradle board upon which she slept during her infancy. Mrs Brant understands the English language but will not speak it.

'They have a fine family of children, one son in particular who resembles his mother in looks and his father in character. He is a good scholar and at an early age a good hunter. When he was only eight years old he followed the trail of a deer far away from his home, and when he became chilled from the cold he built a fire to warm himself and then found his way to his home.

'Joseph Brant has a fine hand-organ which he uses to entertain his guests. He also serves rum, brandy and port every Sunday after he and Mrs Brant attend church.

'They speak fluently in their native tongue, in soft, musical and harmonious voices. Warriors are often called in to entertain guests by doing the War Dance, their clothes glittering with silver of all shapes and forms. Most of the time Captain Brant beats the drums and joins in the singing.

'Captain Brant is very proud of his presents from noblemen in England – a silver-hilted dagger and a gun which fires fifteen shots in the space of half a minute.'

It was in honour of Captain Brant that the Mohawk Chapel and the Mohawk Institute were built in the Brantford area.

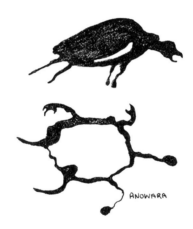

ANOWARA

It was common knowledge when the Six Nations sold eight hundred and seven acres of land to the people of the town of Brantford for five shillings that the Trading Post would remain for the use of the Native people. This agreement was later ratified by a decision of the Court of Chancery.

It was customary for the Native people to take farm produce, wood and axe handles to sell to their white neighbours at the Trading Post. Many of the storekeepers on Colborne Street bought large blocks of wood for their furnaces, and the white women bought homemade quilts, mats, wild fruit in season, butter and eggs.

THE CURSE OF THE MARKET SQUARE

An elderly chief had taken a load of hay to the Trading Post, and he was asked to pay market fees before he could sell his hay. When he refused to do this, he was taken into custody.

Now when the Confederacy was ordained, the Native people had accepted the message of Peace and Goodwill and had buried all their war weapons under the Tree of Peace. But even the wild creatures of the forests have methods of protecting themselves, as the simple tree-toad, when hunted, changes its colour to match its hiding place. The Native people decided to use the only weapon left to them. They had no alternative but to resort to witchcraft and put a curse on the Market Square and all coveted Native land.

The talented Witchcraft Society travelled many miles on the Witches' trail, which finally led to a century-old abandoned log house. Within its walls lies the craft of destruction. It is there permanently, for action when required. Not many people have the gift to operate this craft, and if the person who has prepared a curse dies, it becomes impossible for anyone to undo it.

Under the curse placed on the Brantford Market Square, no one other than a Native can live on the Square, to prosper or even to have a clear mind.

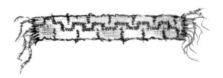

James Kerby, a white man who was interested in fair play for the Natives, took legal action to have all the buildings removed which had been erected on the Market Square. He secured a court decision that 'the Municipality of the town of Brantford had no authority to deal with this as ordinary property of the Corporation.'

On the 8th day of November 1858, a decree concerning the Market Square was made as follows —

In Chancery,

These are to certify that a decree was made by the Court of Chancery for Upper Canada on the eight day of November 1858 in a certain cause therein depending where in Her Majesty's Attorney General for that part of Canada formerly called Upper Canada on behalf of Her Majesty's Informant and the Municipality of the Town of Brantford. George Watt, William Hunter, Thomas Fair, John Aston Wilkes, James Woddyatt, Henry Wade, Philip Cady VanBrocklin, William Sutton, William Morris, Thomas B. Hull, Edmund Brockington and Thomas Robson defendants.

Whereby the said court did declare that the piece of land called the West Market Square in the pleadings mentioned situate in the Town of Brantford, was laid out and dedicated by Her Majesty's Government for the sole purpose of a Market Square to be used for Market purposes only and ought to be kept open and free from any erections or buildings thereon other than for Market purposes and doth order and decree the same accordingly and this court doth further declare that the leases thereof in the pleadings mentioned granted by the Municipality of the Town of Brantford were in Contravention of such dedication and were so made and granted without authority and did order and decree the same accordingly, and the said Court did further order and decree that no renewal of any or either of the leases in the pleadings mentioned should be granted nor any further or other lease of the said premises or any part thereof given nor any buildings or erection placed upon the said premises other than those already thereon and those erected or to be erected for market purposes and that at the determination of the leases heretofore granted by the said Municipality of Brantford the buildings now upon the said premises which have been erected under or by virtue of such leases respectively be forthwith removed so that the said premises may be forever used and enjoyed by the inhabitants of the Town of Brantford free from any such erection or obstruction other than those erected or to be erected for Market purposes, and this Certificate is given at the request of the Plaintiff for the purpose of registration.

Given under my hand and the seal of the said Court this seventh day of February A.D. 1859
(Seal)

S. D. A. GRANT (REGISTRAR)
Registry Office Co. of Brant
Official Copy No. — 2155

I certify that the within Instrument is duly entered and registered in the Registry Office for the Registry Division, County of Brant, in Book D for the Town of Brantford at 12 o'clock of the 9th day of February A.D. 1859

T. Shenston
Registrar of the Co. of Brant

OMENS AND VISIONS

In 1924 the Hereditary Council of Chiefs was replaced by an Elective Band Council as the governing body on the Six Nations Reserve. Previously, the Six Nations had been a sovereign, treaty-making state, with a constitution of its own. Now the people were to be subject to the white man's law under the Indian Act of the Canadian government.

It has been predicted that 'those who undermine the ancient Confederacy shall vomit blood.' Thus many non-Indians have lost their lives on Native land.

The Native people of the Six Nations who were instrumental in destroying the Confederacy and promoting the new system have also gone to the Happy Hunting Ground, most of them in the prime of life.

OKWARI

Dr Peter Martin, whose Native name was O-ronh-ya-deh-ha (meaning burning cloud), was the founder of an international benevolent organization. He had three sisters who were actresses: Lizzie, Maggie and Emma. Whenever they were near their hometown of Brantford, Ontario, they went home to Martin's Corner on the Six Nations Reserve.

It was on one of his visits home that Dr O-ronh-ya-deh-ha had a disturbing dream. In his dream he stood beside the Grand River. He felt good to be there; the river was so peaceful he could see the bottom. Stretching for six miles on each side of the Grand River was a crop of wheat, tall, straight and ready for the harvest. His heart was filled with thanksgiving, for the wheat would make flour for his people.

Suddenly he saw an object in the distance moving towards him. It was a huge machine, and as it moved slowly along it covered six miles on each side of the Grand River. When it passed where he was standing, the ground had become barren, the wheat had all disappeared.

He sat on the ground and covered his face with his hands. He did not know how long he stayed that way, but when he looked up again, he jumped to his feet. For six miles on each side of the Grand River there was a field of corn, tall and straight, swaying gently in the breeze.

The corn was beckoning to someone. He looked around and could see no one, so he walked closer to the field. The corn opened a pathway, and as he walked in he could hear many voices, but he could not see anyone. It gradually became plain to him that the corn was speaking its own native tongue. He realized that the conversation was about the Native people and the terrible things that were coming for them.

Then he saw another vision: It was a Native mother making feeble attempts to transfer some of the heat from her body into the shivering body of her dying infant. The helpless mother watched her baby die. Far off, the lonely cry of a wolf sounded loud and clear and a voice said, 'Another Indian has died.'

The scene before him shifted. A once proud and mighty nation was now being driven from its land. The people were being forced at gunpoint to leave their homes and everything they held dear.

Men were seized in the fields, women were taken from their homes, children were taken from their play and all their homes went up in flames.

Once more he covered his face, and his whole body shivered. Someone touched him on the shoulder, and he opened his eyes to see that the corn was gone. The Grand River was still there, but its waters were not clear any more; they were black with the blood of his people. The weeping willow growing on the banks tried in vain to cover the horrible scene with its branches.

This was the dream of the great doctor, who had been to far-off places, had crossed the waters to England and had been a guest of the Royal Family. His people, the Six Nations, were foremost in his mind. To them, his dream is like a jigsaw puzzle of many pieces; each year a piece falls into place, and soon the puzzle will be completed.

THE CHURCH BELL

It was a beautiful summer night as three young Native men sat on the bank of the Grand River, waiting for two others who were walking home from the city.

They were talking and laughing, when they heard voices which seemed to be coming from the ground. The voices were using the Mohawk language. Behind the three men, and over the fence, was a cemetery, and on a nearby knoll stood a Christian church, where Native people who had been Christianized attended.

The conversation of these invisible voices continued: they were planning something they were about to do. The three young men decided to leave at once, and when they were about a mile away, the church bell began to ring, loud and clear. It was three o'clock in the morning.

The next evening these boys met their friends at a crossroad, and they talked about what had happened the night before. The two boys who had been returning from the city told the other three that something had happened to them as well.

They had been not far away when they heard the church bell ringing. When they reached the church, the lights were on in the basement. They looked through the window and saw people walking around. One of the boys whispered, 'We should go in. They may serve lunch.' The other boy suggested they should see first if they could recognize someone. One boy thought he recognized his grandmother — but she had been dead for some time. The bell kept on ringing. They recognized several people who were dead. Then the lights in the basement went out and the bell stopped ringing.

They had just finished telling their friends about their weird experience when they all heard the church bell ringing again. The boys jumped up and said to each other, 'Come on, there are five of us and we're all alive. We can fight the dead!'

They began to run. The church was about a mile and a quarter away. When they arrived, there were no lights, but the bell kept on ringing. They ran into the room where the sexton rings the bell for church services or funerals. The rope to the bell was gone. Someone would have to climb the ladder that led to the balcony to stop the bell from ringing. Two of the boys went up, and when they reached the belfry, they found that the bell rope was securely tied to a beam and the bell was still ringing. It took them a long time to untangle the rope, but finally they let it down, and the three boys down below tied it where they had seen the sexton secure it.

The bell stopped ringing. The boys walked back to the crossroad and sat down. One of them told a story he had heard from his father about a time before he himself was born.

His father had had a friend, a boy his own age, and they always went out together. His friend had lived not far from this same church, and one night when the boys were walking home, they had heard an angry bull behind them. The bull came closer, and in spite of their running as fast as they could, it was gaining on them. They ran to an old snake rail fence and each got a rail to fight the bull. It came running and passed where they were standing without seeing them, even though it was a moonlit night.

Exactly one month from that night, one of the boys died and was laid to rest in the cemetery by the river.

The young man had just finished the story narrated by his father when they heard the bell ringing again, but they did not return to the church.

Within a month, one of the boys was laid to rest in that same cemetery. His four friends stood together by the graveside and whispered that the bell must have been ringing for him.

UNDISCOVERED UNIVERSE

Once there was a man who had been a cripple all his life. He had no relatives to care for him, and since he was old and feeble he knew that he could not go on alone much longer.

One day as he sat on his rocking chair he began to think about the days gone by. His parents had given him the house he lived in, and as he thought back, he could hear his mother as she said in sadness, 'I am going to leave you with no one to take care of you. When you were a little boy, I used to say if you were a good boy you would walk like other boys. But you have been good and that has never happened. I can only urge you not to lose hope, and I will not be too far away to guide your steps.'

As he continued to reminisce, he thought of a boy his own age who had lived near him. They had played together every day and planned what they would do when they grew to be young men. Alas, they had lost touch early in their teens, and the boy had stopped coming to see him.

The crippled man had heard bad rumours about his friend — rumours that he was hardly ever sober and could not hold a job. He wore flashy clothes just like his rough friends. Although good looking and attractive, he did not stay in one place long enough to settle down. Eventually, he married a nice girl, but he stayed with her only briefly and then began to drift again.

Suddenly, the crippled man was roused from his reverie by someone calling his name, 'Peter, come with me.' He arose and his legs were no longer crippled; they felt good, so straight and strong. Again he heard the voice, 'Follow the light ahead of you; we are going away.' The old man did as he was told. He walked towards a light in a doorway. The voice said, 'Jump, Peter, jump.' And he jumped. He felt the cold air as he floated like a bird — through the mysteries of the Undiscovered Universe.

No man had ever been there; it was like looking through a magnifying glass. Wherever he drifted, he could look through this glass on the world he had just left.

Peter wanted most of all to see his parents. He was guided by some supernatural power, and soon he stopped above the cemetery he knew so well. As he looked through the glass, he could see his parents sleeping in their graves with smiles upon their faces. Peter whispered, 'Mother, I can walk.'

Suddenly he was in a different place. The world below looked dreary and barren. There were no trees or rivers, but as he looked closer he saw a footprint in the sand, sometimes faint and then sharp, then stumbling, as if the sand was deep. As Peter looked at the footprints in the sand they seemed so lonely that they reminded him of his own life. Then, as he looked harder through the glass he saw a body, the body of a man he recognized. It was his boyhood friend, and the body was being devoured by hungry wolves.

Suddenly, the scene below changed again, this time to the tavern where his old friend had met his cronies. Through the glass Peter saw not people but scrawny, ugly wolves grabbing the bottles the bartender placed upon the counter.

Peter screamed, 'Let me pray, please let me pray for forgiveness that I was ever sorry for myself. With all my heart I give thanks that I have never in my whole life shared drink with scrawny, greedy wolves.'

The next day a neighbour found Peter at his house in a semi-conscious state. When he was aroused enough to talk, Peter told the neighbour all the things he had seen.

That night the neighbour stayed with Peter until he went to sleep. Later, Peter died in his sleep, and on the day of his funeral the neighbour told the minister what Peter had seen in the Undiscovered Universe.

The minister used this subject for his sermon. Many people came to Peter's funeral. His boyhood friend, an old man himself, sat in the front seat. He knew the lonely footsteps in the sand were his, and he asked himself what would be at the end of the road for him. He hoped it would not be such a dreadful fate.

The minister spoke words of comfort as he knelt beside this man and assured him that there was still time to turn back the footprints in the sand.

After the funeral, this wayward friend spent many hours at Peter's graveside. He could walk and he had good health, but he thought Peter had been a luckier man, for he had not been defiled, and the world's sins had not corrupted him.

VISIONS IN A GLASS OF WATER

There were two sisters in the family, which lived on an Indian reservation. The younger, Irene, was different from other children, and her sister, who was five years older, depended upon her judgement.

When they were young the girls played together, and whenever they had a party Irene foretold the future by looking into a glass of water. Many times she called out to her sister in terror that she could see her favourite doll choking to death. Sometimes they would laugh about it, but usually Irene was serious. This went on throughout their childhood days, and their mother did not pay much attention, thinking it was just the way they played.

Once their neighbour's dog disappeared. The boy who owned the dog was broken-hearted, because he loved the animal very much.

Everybody in the settlement went looking for the dog, but with no success. That evening at dinner, Irene looked into her glass of water and cried out, 'I see the dog. A man has him on a leash and is kicking him because the dog is trying to get away from him.' Her father remarked to his wife that the girl should go to bed, since the excitement of the day had upset her.

Her sister spoke up. 'She really does see the dog, like all the other things she sees in her glass of water.' She turned to Irene and asked her if she could see anything else. Irene said she knew where the man was with the dog right at that moment, and her sister ran out to tell the neighbour.

They all went in a car, with Irene showing the way. They travelled many miles, then they saw a car with a flat tire. When they stopped to help, the dog, which was chained to the back seat, heard their voices and started to bark. The little boy ran to the dog and hugged it, delighted to have found his pet.

When the sisters became teenagers, they often attended parties given by the community where they lived. One night at one of these parties, Irene's sister met a man who was very nice to her. He never left her side all evening. When the family got home that night, they talked about the party, and the question of this stranger came up. No one knew who he was or where he had come from.

He called to see Irene's sister the next evening and every evening after that. He never talked about himself, and the parents cautioned their daughter, because they knew that she liked him very much.

One night after the man went home, the girl announced their engagement. When questioned, she said she did not know anything about him except that she loved him, and that was enough for her.

That night Irene cried herself to sleep. She had a feeling something terrible was going to happen.

In the morning at breakfast, there was no conversation. Each person seemed under a strain. The mother, in deep thought, was startled when Irene cried out, 'Sister, don't do it, please. I see everything. Listen to me.' The family stopped eating and the mother said, 'Tell us, dear, what do you see?' Irene stared into her glass of water and said, 'That man is older than our father; he has been married many times; the name he is using is not his own. Far away from here I see his wife and little children, shabbily dressed, begging from people for food. I see a trail where this man has been. Dotted along his pathway are little babies, crying pitifully, and some are lying dead. I see two women fighting; each claims to be the wife of this man. Please, sister, don't do it.'

No one spoke. The sister went to Irene and put her arms around her, saying, 'Irene, I have believed your visions in the water since we were children. I have always depended upon your wise judgement and I cannot disregard your judgement today. It is true we know nothing of this man. No, Irene, I will not marry him.'

THE YOUNG NATIVE

A daring young brave of the Six Nations wanted answers to many things — questions like: What lies behind the horizon? What happens when the sky comes down to meet the earth? And if you could stand close enough to run through before the sky came down, what would be on the other side?

He talked to many people, but no one knew the answers to his questions. He made a vow that one day he would find them. He talked to an old chief, who told him to be careful and that he should be satisfied with his life. He warned the young Native that when one is restless and dissatisfied, only the devil knows all the answers. The young man thought for a few days, then he decided he had to see Satan himself, so he visited an old wizard and told him what he wanted.

The old wizard told him to take a piece of the root he gave him and put it in his mouth, hold a jack of spades in his hand, stand at the crossroads and 'wish with all your heart to see the devil.'

He went at midnight and stood at the crossroads, wishing with all his might to see the devil. He did not wait too long. He was startled by the rattling of chains, and the strong odour of sulphur almost took his breath away. When this cleared away he could see Satan himself, complete with long ears, horns, a spear for a tail and a horse's hoofs for feet. He said, 'I heard you call. What do you want?'

The young man could not remember what he wanted, so he said, 'I want to know where you are and to be able to see you at any time.'

The devil answered, 'Go to the cemetery and find the grave of a righteous person. Dig down and get a piece of wood from his casket. Then, wherever you go with your piece of casket wood, look through the keyhole. If I am there you will see me.' Then the devil vanished.

The first place the young man went was to a dance. He looked through the keyhole and saw the devil weaving in and out among the dancers, taking the girls around the waist, swinging his tail and having a good time.

Someone told the young man about an evening service at a local church, and although he did not think he would find the devil in there, he went to see. When he looked through the keyhole of the church, the minister was giving a sermon and there were two pious ladies whispering to one another and pointing to a poorly-clad woman sitting ahead of them. And there was old Satan sitting between the two ladies, reaching up now and again to kiss their cheeks.

Next, the young man went to a bar. The place was full of people, and looking through the keyhole he saw elderly people staggering around the bar with wet chins and clammy hands, drinking and keeping time to the strains of music coming from a ballroom where the young people danced. The young man could see Satan going from one old man to another, slapping them on the back in approval. Many children were also present, and their parents were showing them the way to destruction. For every second glass from the bar, Satan put a number on the parent's forehead and said, 'You shall be called by your number for your last drink of molten lead.'

The young man had seen enough; he wanted to return the wood to the casket. Then he heard a voice, though he saw no one. The voice said, 'Go home, boy, to where you belong; go home to the faith of your fathers.' The wood from the casket disappeared from his hand.

NEW FESTIVALS

OHKWAHO

JERRY

Jerry was eight years old. He went to school every day, and his main interest was his studies. He was liked by his teacher, who said he was a born leader.

Jerry was the only child of hard-working parents. Their house was on the edge of a dense forest. Behind the house was a stream, where many animals would come to drink. Jerry made friends with the animals and often visited them when going though the forest.

One day the teacher announced that there was to be a school concert and asked Jerry to be the bandleader. Jerry played the drums very well, and three other boys also played musical instruments. The teacher named the band 'Cat Rag Band' and told the boys they would need cat costumes. The boys were very excited and decided to ask their parents to make the outfits. Jerry was happy with his finished costume, as it was like the persian kitten he played with near his home.

One day after school Jerry went to the woods in his cat costume. He met four stray cats, but instead of being friendly they spat at him and prepared to fight. Jerry tried talking to them, but they were uncertain and not ready to accept him. He took off his cat uniform, then turned to his cat friends, talking to them and petting them. Finally, they were convinced he was their old friend and they began to purr.

Just at that moment Jerry began to think about the possibility of training the cats to take part in the school concert. Knowing it would be useful, he picked a plant which could be used to influence a cat's behaviour.

Jerry went to see the other three boys who were in the Cat Rag Band and told them his ideas, asking that his plans be kept secret so that on the day of the concert everyone would be surprised. His friends agreed, and they all went off to the woods to find the cats.

When rehearsals were going well, one afternoon the boys took their cat costumes with them so the real cats would get used to them. The costumes were put on, and when the cats no longer mistrusted Jerry or his friends, they all sang and purred together.

The next day Jerry prepared the cat medicine by boiling the special leaves until he got a clear liquid, then adding two spoonsful of sugar. He mixed this well and added it to some milk. He set off for the forest, hoping the cats would be influenced by the mixture so as not to quarrel and fight, but to obey his commands.

The cats drank the medicine. The boys started their music, and the cats meowed while Jerry kept time. When it was over, the boys clapped their hands and the cats jumped on Jerry, washing his face with their rough tongues.

The next problem was how to get the cats to go to the concert. Every day now the boys took a canoe to the woods to practise with the cats. The cats were used to the costumes and would jump into the canoe and meow with the boys. As the school was near the stream, the problem of getting the cats to the concert was solved. The cats loved riding in the canoe with Jerry and the boys.

On the night of the concert the school was filled with people. Finally the Cat Rag Band was announced. There was only silence. Then in the distance the people heard music. It came closer and became louder. Finally, the door opened and the Cat Rag Band marched in. The teacher was very surprised — there had only been four cats; now there were eight in the band!

The Cat Rag Band played three numbers, and when they finished, the people were shouting and clapping. The four real cats jumped on Jerry, washing his face with their rough tongues.

After the last number had been played, all the cats marched out and back to the canoe.

TAWISTAWIS

From the time of Captain Joseph Brant, the Mohawks of the Six Nations acknowledged the white man's New Year. The beginning of a new era was very special to the Natives. The people began their celebration on New Year's Eve.

Relatives and friends gathered together to welcome the New Year. There were house dances, where there were waltzes and square dancing, and there was also a prize for the best step-dancer. The ladies brought their New Year's baking: roast goose, sandwiches, cookies with the stamp of the New Year, pies, pound cakes and many gingerbread dolls.

In various parts of the reservation, undenominational religious services were held. The people sang sacred hymns translated into the Mohawk language. Natives came from other reservations like Caughnawaga, Oneida, St Regis and Oka to attend these religious services. The minister in charge was a Mohawk and spoke in his native tongue.

At the stroke of midnight everybody stood up and held hands while the Indian choir sang in their native tongue, 'Let Us Love One Another.' After this, everybody shook hands and cried 'Noh-yarh,' which meant 'Happy New Year.'

The first day of the year was Children's Day. They were up early in the morning, all wrapped up in woollens to go from house to house shouting, 'Noh-yarh.' They were given New Year's baking, candies, oranges and apples, and they all carried large bags to put their goodies in. These children walked for miles, the smaller ones drawn on hand sleighs.

The older men were watching their polished snow snakes glide swiftly through the trenches they had made. They were competing to see which snow snake could travel the farthest. The speed depended on the temperature of the track and the wax polish they made themselves. All this required great skill.

In the evening, the teenagers and young married people had skating parties on the largest ponds, with dozens of kerosene lanterns hanging from tree branches.

THE OLD YEAR

One New Year's Eve, just before dusk, a man and his wife were gliding along in their horse-drawn cutter to attend a New Year's Eve celebration with their parents. They were driving along the river, and the snow was piled up along the sides of the road. Suddenly the wife cried, 'Stop! See a man's hand sticking out of the snowbank beckoning to us!' Her husband stopped the sleigh and went to investigate. It was, indeed, a man's hand. They called some neighbours to come and help, and they shovelled all the snow away to find that it was an elderly man with long white hair. No one knew him, but they put him in a bob-sleigh drawn by horses and took him to the nearest hospital. He was pronounced dead on arrival at the hospital, and his rescuers never found out who he was. The county buried him in a nearby cemetery.

This incident had not been forgotten when New Year's Eve came around again. The same couple was driving to the traditional roast goose dinner when the woman cried out, 'Stop! There is the man's hand again!' Instead of getting out, they drove to a neighbour's for help. When they shovelled all the snow away, they found it was the same elderly man as the year before. They were a little nervous and all went together to get a man with a bob-sleigh to take the man to the hospital. When they returned with the bob-sleigh, the elderly man was gone, but the imprint of his body was there in the snow-drift.

THEKAHON

Hallowe'en was a time when the small children were allowed by their parents to go with other children and just have fun, but they all had to be back at home by ten o'clock, just before the magic Hand flies in the air looking for disobedient children.

The children loved to decorate neighbours' gates with twigs and leaves. Some of them made large rag dolls and filled them with dry grass and leaves. Then they placed the dolls here and there along the road.

When the young children were safely home, the older people had their turn to have fun. No women were allowed to go, because the young boys liked to travel many miles through fields and over ditches on Hallowe'en.

A MEETING WITH OLD NICK

One Hallowe'en night a group of about twenty-five young men went out together. They were talking, laughing and singing as they went along, exchanging the farmers' gates and putting black pigs with the neighbours' white ones.

They sat down on the ground to cool off and plan their next move. The night was young and the moon was full.

One of the boys called out, 'Somebody tell us a story, a scary ghost story.' One of them answered, 'I will tell a story, but if you see anything, please don't run and leave me.' Everybody laughed at that remark. 'Go ahead and tell the story; we won't leave you. Who's afraid of a Hallowe'en ghost?'

The young man began his story by telling about the time the church was being repaired. The workers had only two days to finish, because a service was to be held on the third day.

The moon was bright, almost like day, as the group of young men listened to the story-teller.

'The men were working at night. The church had electric lights, and suddenly, high up on a beam, the workers could see the figure of a little man hardly three feet high, with a spear at the end of his tail. The figure was waving to and fro as if to jump.'

The boys crept closer to each other. Suddenly one of them said, 'Stop the story. Jack is cracking up with fright.' They all turned to look at Jack. He was staring straight ahead, and as they followed his gaze they saw a huge figure approaching.

This enormous thing was dark in colour, and they could hear a hissing sound as it kept on coming towards them. They all jumped to their feet, but the 'thing' covered each of them. They were standing close together, but when it covered them they could not see one another.

The young man who was telling the story was a 'life-of-the-party' and he was not afraid of anything. He had a small twenty-two revolver with him and he shot it up into the air. The 'thing' vanished but immediately returned.

The boys started to run towards their homes. They ran quickly, but the black cloud was right behind them. The story-teller got his gun and shot again; the 'thing' disappeared. They ran as fast as they could, but soon the cloud was coming again. The young man said, 'The next time I shoot, run to the nearest farmhouse.' They did this.

Meanwhile, all the dogs in the neighbourhood had heard the shots and came running to the scene. The boys could hear the dogs fighting the 'thing.' Since they knew they could frighten it away with gunshots, the boys decided to make torches and go out there and help the dogs.

The boys ran with their torches towards where the dogs were fighting. They could not see what happened, but suddenly the dogs just stopped barking and dropped to the ground, panting. The 'thing' was gone.

The men examined the dogs. There were no bites or scratches, but each one had a peculiar odour. It smelled as though it had been sprayed with sulphur.

Gilbert was a ghost, who according to the legend, sat on the west bridge near Ohsweken, Ontario, a village which is the capital of the Six Nations territory.

Many people had seen the ghost as he sat on the edge of the cement bridge in all his transparent whiteness, with his bony hands stretched out.

A man who was walking home from Brantford saw Gilbert on the bridge one night. The man had heard about the ghost, but had doubted the story. He decided that this was a good time to find out whether Gilbert was a real ghost. Certainly, many people had been frightened to the point where they did not go out at night any more.

The man noticed that the apparition was transparent and that he could see the guard rail of the bridge through it. As he walked closer, he noticed that the ghost was crunching on something. When he drew near, the ghost slowly turned and the man saw, to his surprise, that the ghost was a skeleton. It had large holes for eyes and its skinless face was grinning. At its feet was a large pile of apple cores, and it was stretching out its bony hands.

The ghost was evidently begging for apples. The man said, 'Sorry, old boy, I do not have any apples.' At that instant the ghost picked up the apple cores and showered the man, hitting him on the face and head with such terrific force that the man jumped over the ditch and the fence and ran as fast as he could. Even so, the apples kept on coming.

The man remembered a house which stood back in the field, and he could see a light. He pounded on the door, but there was no answer. Finally, he forced his way in and found an elderly woman sitting at a table. When she saw him she jumped up, grabbed the broom and hit him hard on the side of his head. Then he remembered that the woman was stone deaf and could not understand what he was trying to tell her.

He got a piece of paper out of his pocket and drew a picture of the bridge and the skeleton while she looked on. Then she ran and locked the door and asked him not to leave her.

After hearing about this experience, children and teenagers were afraid to be out at night.

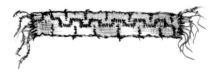

Another traveller had a flat tire a short distance away from the bridge. The moon was bright and he did not think he would have any trouble changing it. There was no one around as he got out of the car. He took the tire off and put on the spare from the trunk. As he put on the tire, someone handed him the bolts. He was nearly finished before he realized that he should be alone. Who, then, was handing him the things he required? He looked up to see the ghost helping itself from a basket of apples in the car. The man was frightened, but he reached for the basket of apples and offered it to Gilbert. The ghost took the basket with his long bony fingers, and the man jumped in the car and drove as fast as he could to his home. The next day he drove past the bridge, and the empty basket was there.

THE GHOST AND THE HAND

Gilbert the Ghost had been frightening the Natives of Grand River for many years. He travelled throughout the country in a variety of disguises. Most of the time he was just a skeleton begging for apples; in another district, he rode a bicycle in his skeleton form; and sometimes on a lonely road, he walked as a well-dressed, prominent man with no head on his shoulders.

The neighbours were asking one another what to do about this apparition which was frightening them so often.

Gilbert went his limit when he attacked a teenage boy who was returning from the city slightly under the influence of firewater. He saw the skeleton sitting on the bridge, and when he got near enough he threw stones at it, yelling, 'Come on and fight, you bony coward.'

Gilbert seemed to be surprised. No one had ever dared to shout at him; he would teach this young man a lesson. He jumped up and grabbed the boy and would have killed him if the Hand had not come to his rescue.

The Hand flew in a circle and slapped Gilbert with a terrific force, knocking off one of his arms. Then it made another circle, and the teenager fell to the ground. As he lay there, unable to get up, he saw the Hand demolish the skeleton. Bit by bit, its bones were scattered all over the road. Each piece, when it landed upon the ground, shivered and twitched and slowly vanished.

Gilbert the Ghost is now a thing of the past and has not been seen for many years. But the Hand is still on patrol for wayward children. He sleeps during the daylight hours and is wide awake at night.

THE SPOOKY ROAD

One evening a man and his wife were driving home from the city in a horse and buggy when they met an elderly woman carrying a small basket. Suddenly she walked out in front of them. They looked to see where she had gone, but she had disappeared completely. The horse was so frightened it almost ran away.

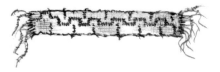

On another occasion, at this same spot, four young people returning to the city heard a dog barking under their buggy. The driver stopped and everybody got out. The dog kept on barking, but they could see nothing.

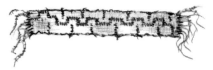

Another time, two people were walking to the Native settlement when they decided to sit by the side of the road for a little rest. They could hear a truck coming, so they stood up with the hope of getting a ride. As the truck passed, one of its tires went flat and the truck stopped. The two people ran towards it, but the truck disappeared.

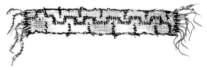

One day a teenager missed her ride from the city, so she walked home. It was almost midnight. She noticed a lady in white walking behind her. When the teenager walked fast so did the lady in white. When she stopped to try to talk to her, the lady in white stopped as well. The teenager was frightened. The houses were far apart and she could see no lights. She remembered an old log house near the edge of the reservation and planned to go there for help.

She turned off the road, walking towards the house. The gate was closed and had wire around the post to keep it closed. She unfastened the wire. . . . The lady in white still stood behind her. As she ran up to the house and pounded on the door, the lady in white fastened the gate.

No one answered the door. The girl tried to get back to the road, but the gate was fastened so tightly she could not unfasten it. The lady in white was right behind her, and she fell to the ground in terror.

It was daylight when the bachelor came home. He found the girl lying by his gate, and he had to cut the wire before he could get into his yard.

The older people said a woman had been murdered by her husband on this road.

THE HAUNTED HOUSE

A man, his wife and their two-month-old baby moved into a small house in the country. In this particular community, the houses were from one-half to one mile apart.

The house had two rooms downstairs and one large room upstairs, and someone had removed the stairs. It was late when the family moved in, so they put up a bed in the front room for the night. So it would be possible for them to go upstairs, the man would begin making a stairway the next day.

Sometime during the night the woman was awakened by a noise. She listened for a second and discovered that the noise was coming from the upstairs bedroom. She awakened her husband and they listened. Someone was rocking in a chair just above their bed.

When they had rented the house, they had been told no one had lived in it for many years. But they wondered if someone, perhaps a hobo, could have been upstairs when they moved in. It had been impossible to look.

The house had no electricity, and they had only kerosene lamps, so they decided to wait until daylight to see what was making the

noise. When they got up in the morning, they could still hear the chair rocking.

The man and woman moved the table to where the stairs would go and placed a wooden box on top. The man poked his head through the opening and was able to see a rocking chair, rocking without anyone sitting in it. There were some long dresses and winter coats, all on hangers, several pairs of shoes and a sewing basket.

That day the man began to build the stairs, but he did not finish by nightfall. The family slept downstairs again. Once more they heard rocking and, this time, someone walking around above their heads.

They were up early, as the man was determined to finish the stairs and solve the mystery. In the afternoon the couple went upstairs, leaving the baby in her crib. They found an old cupboard, but there was no food in it. All the time they were upstairs the chair kept rocking. The man took the chair and laid it on its side.

His wife cried out, 'Look at these dresses.' They both saw the dresses swaying back and forth. The man saw a bony hand sticking out of the sleeve of one of the dresses. He said quickly, 'Let's go downstairs. It's time to feed the baby.' He hoped his wife had not seen the bony hand. He told her to go down first and he would walk behind her. They were halfway down when they heard a loud noise. Someone had picked up the rocking chair and was rocking in it again.

The man told his wife to grab the baby and he would take them somewhere to spend the night. He would find someone to stay the night with him at this strange house, as he wanted to find out about the unusual activities upstairs. His wife did not want to go, but when he told her about the bony hand she no longer argued.

As they left the house they heard more noise upstairs. The man was glad to get his wife and child out before harm came to them.

He took his family a mile away to a neighbour's house. Six men volunteered to go back with him. All carried kerosene lanterns, and it was dark when they got to the house. They heard the rocking chair and decided to go upstairs and throw everything outside.

The first man who went up had a hand pushed in his face. The battle did not last long. Five of the men collapsed as if under a drug; the sixth man ran out to contact the owner. Five men had to have medical attention and were found to be under hypnosis.

News of what had happened soon spread. An old woman came to see the young couple and told them what she knew about the mystery.

The woman who had lived in the house had been a bad woman. When she became ill and was told she would die, she refused to believe it and would not repent of her sins. She warned that she would haunt people after she died and that anyone who crossed her path would be put to sleep.

The young family was never able to live in the house, and shortly after their experience it burned to the ground.

LIVING TRADITIONS

Among the Native people of today there is still a strong feeling for the traditional values. The ancient religion lives on, and the myths and legends of the past find repeated expression in the everyday life of the people.

One practical belief is that a person will be treated according to the way he treats others. Even the food brought into the house is given by the Creator and is to be shared with whoever wants it. Thus food is always offered to strangers who are in the house at mealtimes.

The loyalty of a Native, once obtained, can be relied upon. He is known for keeping his word.

Prayer plays a large part in the life of a Native settlement. The people pray with humility to the Creator to remember their needs, to guide them on a journey or through an ordeal, to comfort them in hard times, to give good conditions for the crops.

They give thanks at sowing time in the spring, at the height of the growing season and again at the harvest. They give thanks for a child when it is born. They give thanks for their knowledge of nature, which enables them to live in harmony with the land.

KARAKONHA

A Native — a cobbler by trade — had become dissatisfied with his life. He disliked everything and everybody, and his business, which had been flourishing at one time, was now very slow. The whole world looked dark and gray.

One day, while alone in his shop, he began to think of his parents, long gone to their rest. He remembered the good Christian upbringing they had given him in a nice home, and he covered his face with his hands and wept.

Suddenly he heard a wailing, of wind or a voice . . . he listened. . . . It was not the wind nor a voice, but heavenly music softly playing. The melody was a hymn he had often heard his mother sing, 'Shall We Gather at the River.'

He looked around; the music was still playing. It seemed to be coming from one corner of his shop. He quickly moved away the boxes that had accumulated with the passing years, and there, covered with dust and grime, was his mother's old harp, still playing the melody he loved so well.

He picked up the harp and held it close to him, and it seemed as if his mother's presence was in the room. He saw the events of his life unfold like pages in a book, and he saw the well-trodden path to the saloon where he left his worries and troubles, together with the respect he once had. He saw the loved ones who had cared about him, and they looked sad; the harp was playing 'God be With You Till We Meet Again.'

This magic harp had awakened the good seeds his parents had planted in his soul. He cleaned his shop, decorated his windows and put up a new sign in the front of his store —

> Everybody is welcome,
> Come one, come all,
> Come with a smile.

Neighbours gathered together and talked in whispers. This man was so mean to everybody, they wondered if he had gone mad. As they stood talking, they heard the wonderful strains of 'Shall We Gather at the River' coming from the cobbler's shop.

Soon there was a crowd of people in front of the shop singing the old hymns, while the good neighbours brought baskets of food so that they might eat together to celebrate this wonderful occasion.

HE BECAME A FROG

There once was a man who lived in an Indian settlement. He did not like people to visit him, and most of all he disliked children. Their parents warned them not to go near his place; they were afraid he might harm them.

One day some Native children did go to his place, mostly out of curiosity. He was in the house cooking his dinner. The children stood at the door, and one forward little boy went inside.

The man turned and saw the children. He grabbed his soup ladle and started hitting them until all the children had fled. He slammed the door, locking the little boy inside his house.

The children were screaming as they ran through the forest. One of the Little People heard their cries and approached them to find out what had frightened them. After they told her about the man and how he had kept the little boy, the fairy went quickly to his house. She knocked on the door, but there was no answer. She heard sobbing, then a scream and a loud thump on the floor. She mumbled to herself, 'Someone needs to be taught a lesson.' Using her magic wand she walked through the door and found the man hitting the boy. She quickly raised her wand and, waving it over the man's head, commanded, 'Hop! you are now a frog; hop for your life before the serpent devours you.'

At that instant, the man turned into a frog. His head-dress with one feather fell to the floor. With his frog arms he tried to put it

154

back on, but he now had a frog's head and the head-dress would not fit.

He became very excited and began hopping about. He could not reach the table, but the thought of food made him ill anyway. It was now flies and insects he craved. It was growing dark and chilly. Unable to close the door, he just flopped on the floor and went to sleep.

Early the next morning he awoke and thought he had had a bad dream and wondered why his door was open. Suddenly he remembered: yesterday he was a man and he could talk. Now he was no bigger than a pancake — he was a frog. He remembered the children standing at the door and how angry he had been, and he decided to go away, as he no longer needed his home.

He hopped outside and kept on hopping. In the distance he saw a swamp, and wanting to go for a swim, he hurried to get there. He was surprised to see so many frogs like himself in the water. They were talking and laughing, but he could not understand them, and when spoken to he just looked at them. The frogs formed a group and in the next instant attacked the man-frog. He could not protect himself, as he did not have the fighting tactics of a frog.

All the frogs went away and left him lying there, bruised and panting. If only the children would come along, he thought; maybe they would help him. They were good kids. He remembered the nice dresses they had worn and how they loved to laugh.

The fairy appeared, compassionately looking upon the frog. She asked him if he was hurt. He could not answer, not even to nod his head. She said, 'Now that you have received your punishment for your cruelty to children, I wonder if you have learned your lesson to be kind to everybody. If you have, I will change you back.' The frog looked at the fairy with tears streaming down his frog-face.

The fairy waved her magic wand and declared, 'Frog, frog, be gone.' Immediately the man arose and on bended knee kissed the fairy's hand.

The man had learned his lesson. From that time on he opened his home to all the children in the settlement. He made beautiful toys for them to play with. The children's parents were happy too and wondered what had changed him.

ALICE AND THE SPIDER

Alice was a pretty little girl. She was an only child but was never lonely. There were many things for her to do, like taking care of birds and insects when they were hurt.

Alice's family lived on the outskirts of a large wooded area, and Alice knew the woods very well. She was a friend to everything that lived in the woods.

Some time ago she had rescued a spider which had had broken legs. She had put it in a box and cared for it the best way she knew how. She had also nursed a crow back to health.

The butterflies and birds and all the creatures she had taken care of began to bring other injured creatures to her home. The ones that had been hurt refused to leave her and when frightened flew to her for protection.

The spider was growing larger every day. It followed Alice wherever she went, especially when she went into the woods.

One day a poisonous snake waylaid her. She was trapped and could not escape. The birds and her other friends were twittering excitedly in order to distract the snake's final move.

No one missed the spider or saw what he was doing. He worked underneath the dry leaves on the ground and spun a web around the snake until it could not move. The little girl's life was saved.

Alice's parents were concerned that the spider was becoming so huge, but somehow they knew it would never hurt her.

One day a vicious stray dog attacked Alice. The spider shoved her to one side and fought the dog. Her parents ran out to see what all the commotion was about and were horrified to see the spider and the dog fighting.

157

The crow was perched on a nearby tree with Alice's other animal friends, watching everything. Her father ran inside to get a gun, but Alice screamed, 'Do not shoot, you might hit the spider.' It did not take long to end the fight. The spider went over to the girl.

In the twinkling of an eye, the huge spider stood up straight, tall and dazzling, like a thousand stars from the heavens. She bowed to Alice and said her mission was accomplished and now she must go to join her friends in the crevices of the rocks.

The spider was a fairy who had been sent to check on the girl's sincerity about poor helpless creatures.

The crow stood on one leg and then the other. The fairy waved her wand, and the crow flew from the tree and hugged Alice. The crow was a fairy too.

THE MAGIC BALL

Eight-year-old Jackie had a small yellow kitten, which had a peculiar ball to play with.

Jackie did not know where the ball had come from. It had appeared one evening when she saw the kitten playing with something underneath her mother's chair. At first she thought the thing was a mouse, but when she took it from the kitten, she saw it was a ball; on it was the picture of a cat, grinning. The kitten took the ball everywhere it went.

Jackie told her mother that every time she looked at the cat's picture on the ball it would blink its eyes. Her mother did not believe this and did not bother to look at the ball.

This fantastic ball was very protective of Jackie and the kitten. One day Jackie went for a walk and the kitten followed her, playing with its ball as it scampered along by her feet.

Soon they came upon three boys who wanted to see the kitten's ball. Jackie let them see it and they ran away with it. She called for them to stop, but they ran all the faster.

She picked the kitten up and began to cry. Just then she heard the boys screaming. They were on the ground, and the ball was bouncing from one to another.

The little girl ran over to them, and the ball bounced back to where the kitten was. The faces of the boys were all scratched and bleeding, and they were screaming as they ran to tell their parents.

Rumour soon spread that Jackie owned a kitten which had a peculiar ball, and crowds of people came to see it. Two young businessmen decided they could make a lot of money with the ball, and they tried many times to buy it, but Jackie always refused.

The men plotted and schemed and finally decided to steal the ball. They went to Jackie's house, and one stayed outside while the other went into the house. He told Jackie he had come to see the ball, which was now very famous. She called the kitten, and the ball rolled along with it. The man picked the ball up with the pretence of examining it, then he threw it outside to his partner.

Jackie tried to go out, but the man blocked her way. Suddenly they could both hear the other man speaking loudly and then screaming for help. They ran outside to see what had happened and found the man on the ground, bruised and bleeding, with the ball biting his nose.

These two men were glad to leave. Jackie, the kitten and the ball lived happily ever after.

THE THIRTEENTH ROOM

An old chief of the Mohawks told a story he had heard from his grandfather about a large house with thirteen rooms. The house was built of logs and a few years later covered with pine boards. Today it stands, stately and graceful, surrounded by tall pine trees which make the rooms almost dark in the daylight.

An elderly couple lived there, a remnant of an old English family who had come to America many years before. The only visitor they ever had was a fourteen-year-old Native boy, who ran errands for them and who stopped by each evening. Sometimes they would just sit in the kitchen and talk about the old days. The boy never went into any other part of the house.

One evening when he made his nightly call, the old man was waiting for him. His wife had become ill and he hoped the boy would stay for the night. He told the boy, whose name was Elmer, that he could sleep on the couch in the front room. The old man would be glad just to know he was there.

It was a beautiful room, with rich old furnishings: the piano with its carved claw-foot legs, the red drapes, the red tapestry tablecloth and matching carpet, the carved love-seat, the cushioned chairs and a grandfather and a grandmother's chair on either side of the fireplace. The boy lay on his couch trying to imagine what the people looked like who had lived here before and what these ancestors of the elderly couple had done for a living.

He was just drifting off to sleep when he was awakened by voices. He went into the hall, knowing the old folks would call him if they needed him, and while he waited he noticed the beautiful oil lamp hanging in the hall. The lamp was red with frosted trimming and glowed softly, giving the boy a peaceful feeling.

Soon the voices died down, and Elmer went back into the living room and slept until morning. Next day, the old gentleman asked him to come and stay again that night. The man's wife was worse and he was very worried. The boy did not say anything about the voices he had heard the night before, and he assured the old man that he would be glad to help them in any way he could. The gentleman smiled and said, 'You have been a great help. It is time we had a talk. When the time is appropriate, I shall call you. Please come at once.'

161

That night, the boy went into the living room and was soon fast asleep. It was towards morning when he heard the voices again. He got up and went into the hall. A door creaked and someone called his name. He ran up the stairs. The old gentleman was standing at an open door beckoning him to go in.

The old lady was lying on a canopied bed with its silk drapes partly drawn. She looked at Elmer and smiled. He quickly went to her bedside and kissed her on the cheek. She thanked him and said to her husband, 'I do not need any more proof. The boy has proved himself worthy. We shall talk tonight. He must know everything.'

That night the old lady told them both to sit close to her bedside. She told Elmer that she and her husband were descendants of an old family and that they had inherited this beautiful home. Since they had no one to hand it down to and no heirs to carry on the traditions of the family, they had chosen him.

She asked him to think about what they had decided to do. He would have to stay with them another night before the old couple would disclose the last and most important part of their suggestion — the conditions concerning the old house. The property would become his very own.

Elmer thanked her and promised to stay again the next night. When he went back, the old man welcomed him as usual. His wife had slept all afternoon, and he told the boy to lie down until he was called.

The night was dark and calm. Just before dawn someone called his name. He hurried into the hall. Again he heard his name. He went up to the old lady's room, where he found the old man sitting by the bed with his head bowed low.

The old lady was talking quickly, as though she was afraid she would not have time to finish. She told the boy the crisis had come.

Long, long ago, a man — a Native — had saved the lives of the old lady's great-great-grandparents. They were very grateful, and when he became ill with a fatal disease, they cared for him. When he was near death, he asked them not to bury him when he died, but to leave him in the thirteenth room of the house, where he kept all his roots and herbs. He told them how to turn his body into stone, so that he would always be in the house to protect the family. When the family became extinct, he would be buried on the same day as his friends, along with everything he owned, which was in the thirteenth room.

His mission of watching over the family was his way of showing his gratitude to them for looking after him.

The old lady said there was one thing more that Elmer should know. Her husband would die the same day as she. As the boy was the new owner of this house, he was to go to the thirteenth room, where he would find two empty coffins and the third with the Native in it.

He must bury them all together, and on the table in that room, in a small box, he would find the papers giving him title to the property.

THE BAD WOMAN

A four-year-old Native girl was injured in an accident, and both of her parents were killed. Her spine was so seriously damaged that she would never walk again. She was sent from one relative to another, the people who looked after her being always well paid.

Her parents had owned a large farm with a big herd of purebred cattle and a beautiful old house furnished with antique furniture. They had always had hired help to do the chores.

One day a woman approached the authorities stating that she was the only legal relative this little girl had. She came prepared to move into the home and had all the required credentials to take full responsibility.

After she moved in, the neighbours did not see the girl any more. They asked the hired help about the girl, but soon the woman fired the workers and sold the cattle. She said that the hired help had quit their jobs and she could not do the chores herself. She claimed to need the money to buy the girl clothes and other things, but she was really saving it for herself.

The little girl did not know this woman and found it difficult to get used to her. She missed her mother's gentle voice and her patience and kindness with everybody. She endured untold hardships; what she could not do for herself she went without. No one gave her a bath before she went to sleep at night, and she no longer had her glass of milk at bedtime. Whenever she became restless, she was severely punished.

The girl was now ten years old. She still could not walk, of course, and her situation seemed quite hopeless to her. She had saved her mother's picture and kept it hidden under her pillow. Each night she got it out and hugged it tightly, saying, 'Mommy, I am so sad and alone, please take me.'

One night after the little girl had talked to her mother's picture, she burst into loud sobs, which caused the woman to go into her room. She saw the picture in the girl's hand, jerked it away from her and tore it to pieces. Then she ran and threw it in the fireplace in the front room and set it on fire. She came rushing back into the girl's room carrying a strap and saying, 'If you are going to stay here with me you are going to do what I say. You are a big girl now and a nuisance to have around. I will teach you my ways or break you.'

Just as she raised the strap to strike the girl, they heard a crackling sound, and the woman opened the door. The next room was filled with smoke, and the flames quickly spread through the house. With horrible screams the woman perished in the flames.

The Little People had many times witnessed the cruelty of this woman, and they had compassion for the little girl. They went into the burning house and carried her outside where she was free from harm.

Firemen and neighbours found the distorted body of the woman but could not locate the girl. They searched the grounds, which they thought was pointless because she could not walk; but at last they

found her — lying near the rose bushes fast asleep, a smile on her face and above her a white dove flying around in a circle.

She was taken to the hospital in an ambulance. There kind doctors volunteered their services to make her well. They performed surgery with prayers and were richly rewarded.

Now the girl is happy. She can walk again and must very seldom remember the painful years of her childhood.

THREE ROSES

A long time ago three solitary roses grew along a dusty road. They felt they were wasting their time by the side of the road. Since it never rained, they were covered with dust, and no one could see their pretty colours.

One day a smartly dressed young man and a very pretty young lady walked along the road on their way to church. The young girl wanted a rose to wear on her dress, and the young man said to her, 'Just a minute; a few steps back I saw three roses growing by the side of the road.' So they turned back. They found the three roses, but the young girl remarked that no one could see their colour, for they were covered with dust. The young man touched one plant and tried to brush off the dust, but it had penetrated right into the bud, which was streaked with the moisture from the early morning dew. 'How pathetic. It looks as if this rose has been crying,' he said, and they walked on without disturbing the plant.

The three solitary roses bemoaned their fate. They knew that roses were supposed to be precious and could not understand why no one ever noticed them. They began to cry. Nearby stood a large oak tree. It had grown accustomed to the roses' constant complaining, and it said to them, 'You see, everybody and everything has been left on this earth for a purpose. People, birds and animals take shelter underneath my branches, and my chest fills with pride as I realize I am needed.

'I can remember, as a little tree, standing here alone. I made it my career to understand my situation. I have been here for centuries and I have witnessed many things. But the most tragic thing I ever saw was the accident in which six young people were killed. They were driving recklessly and were a danger to other drivers. Suddenly the car swerved and turned over. The spirits of the three girls were transferred to three roses.'

Looking down at the roses the tree continued, 'I know why you are here. You are being punished because you have been wayward and inconsiderate. Look closely and see what you have done to my trunk. Your initials are carved so deeply the scars will remain there forever; you have no regard for beauty or for property. You were disobedient to your parents. You even killed my grandson; his life was just beginning when you ended yours to become three dust-laden roses.'

Just as the oak tree finished his story, the skies grew dark, a strong wind came up and a storm broke loose. Thunder and lightning flashed through the skies, and the rain came down in torrents. All the trees in the woods bent low to the ground. Here and there a tree was splintered or blown down by the fury of the storm, but the oak tree stood tall and unshaken, blinded by the flashes of lightning. The storm seemed endless, but it finally subsided just before the break of day. The oak tree looked around and saw that many trees were down. But he could not see the three roses.

The three roses awoke to find themselves in another world, feeling very refreshed, as though they had had a shower. How nice it was to feel so clean! At a distance they saw the oak's grandson. He was almost as tall as his grandfather. They were very happy to see him again.

Suddenly they heard a voice saying, 'I want you to pay strict attention to what I am going to say. At the time of your accident you were transformed into three roses growing along a dusty country road. The reason for this was to give you a chance to redeem yourselves. You are again three beautiful girls, but you cannot return to your families, because they have now ceased grieving over your deaths. You are now between your earthly home and the heavens. This is your final test to atone for your waywardness, grumbling and constant complaining.

In this world you are free to go wherever you like. There are only you three human beings here, and I caution you that this world — unlike the earth, which has solid ground — has clouds, and these clouds have pitfalls. Should you step into a pitfall, you will go down and disappear completely. These pitfalls are caused by disobedience, untruth, malice, vanity and hatred — all qualities which you girls have shown on earth. There are only two things to redeem you: love and faith. I hope you will find the clouds easy to walk upon; love is the greatest of the commandments, and with faith you will never fall.'

THE TRIPLETS

Robert's parents had lost their lives in an accident, and the only relatives the young boy had were his father's three sisters. They were triplets, long past middle age, and were very much alike in every way. When they learned of the death of their only brother and his wife, they decided to go back to the old homestead where they were born and look after their nephew, Robert, for they were all he had now.

Robert's father had often talked about his sisters and how they loved their home in the Native settlement. He had told Robert about the purity of their belief in their old traditions and customs and that they always dressed in Native attire. Although Robert had never seen his aunts, he felt he knew them well and was anxious to meet them. He waited for them in great anticipation.

When they arrived, he marvelled at their great resemblance to his father. They even used the same tone of voice. His heart was touched and he felt sad as he hugged them.

The sisters were pleased with their nephew. After lunch on the day of their arrival, they went to the cemetery and knelt by the graveside of their brother, promising to take care of his son forever.

They did everything for the boy. He almost forgot his own parents, he was so happy. The sisters found interest in everything he did, and they helped him with his school work and loved all his young friends. They were good housekeepers and lived in complete harmony, never contradicting one another. They always attended all the traditional ceremonies and the thanksgiving festivals. The boy was thankful to be a part of this family.

When Robert became a teenager, his three aunts seem to melt into his way of life. They talked about things he liked and kept young by being interested in his activities. Sometimes they would talk about the future in all its dazzling hope.

One day they signed over to Robert all their earthly possessions. These, along with his inheritance from his parents, would insure that he would never be in want. This was a great satisfaction to the sisters, as time was running out for them and they wanted him to be happy.

The day Robert became twenty-one years old, one of his aunts was afflicted with a strange ailment. A specialist was consulted but could do nothing. Then the other sisters fell ill. When one passed away, the other two were already unconscious. Robert went from one to the other saying, 'Please let one live,' but it was not to be. It was soon over, and there were now five graves in the cemetery.

Robert remembered that whenever he and his aunts had talked about death and the Hereafter, they had always told him never to be afraid, for they would never leave him. He found great comfort in remembering the things they had said.

Robert was alone in the house the night after the funeral. It was very dark and still, and the stars outside gave no light. All he heard was the grandfather's clock chiming the midnight hour.

As he walked down the hall toward his room, he saw the three sisters standing outside their bedroom door, dressed in their best native costume, smiling lovingly at him.

He was startled for a second. Then he remembered that they had always said, 'Never be afraid,' so he threw a kiss to them and went on to bed. He was very tired.

When he awoke next morning, the sun was shining brightly, and he felt refreshed. While he was eating his breakfast, the happenings of the evening before came back to him. He did not know how to feel about the situation. He was almost happy to know that his aunts had not really deserted him.

The aunts were there every night and he always threw a kiss to them.

One day Robert met a girl named Irene, who was also an orphan but not as lucky as he. She had been adopted by cruel parents, but as soon as she was old enough the authorities had placed her in a boarding school — a timely escape from her cruel foster parents.

Robert wanted to ask Irene to marry him, but he wondered if he should do so without telling her of the ghostly appearances of his aunts every night. He did not think she would understand.

He had never gone into his aunts' bedroom, but now something seemed to urge him to go. He looked through all their documents and papers and finally found one that interested him. It concerned their nightly appearances and how long they would continue. His aunts had believed that if they loved a person with all their hearts, they would be permitted to be always close to their loved one, even after death. It also stated that the aunts would never leave Robert as long as he was alone, but should he marry a girl he loved, they would leave and stay in their last resting place, biding their time until loved ones meet again.

That night he went to see Irene and told her about his three aunts, how wonderful they had been to him after his parents died and what had happened that night after the funeral and every night after that.

Robert gave the document to Irene to read, and with tear-filled eyes, she assured him that although her love for him was only from one person, it would equal the love of his three aunts.

After they were married, Robert took Irene to see his aunts' room. As he opened the hall door, the three aunts were at the end of the hall, smiling radiantly as they waved their last good-bye.

TOM AND TED

Tom and Ted were close neighbours who lived on an Indian settlement. Their parents loved them very much.

Their summer holidays were just about over, and like all boys, they did not want to go back to school. The two boys often created problems for their parents, but since neither boy had brothers or sisters, their parents never reprimanded them. As they grew older, the problems became more serious.

As soon as they were old enough to walk, the boys began to torment or destroy whatever came their way. They smashed all their toys. Their parents tried to buy toys which would hold their interest, but this would only work for a little while. They killed all the cats and dogs in the neighbourhood. As they grew older, everyone disliked them. They were not invited to any parties, because they fought with the other girls and boys. The parents of the boys always made excuses for their actions.

One day just before Tom and Ted were to start school, they went into the woods looking for adventure. They chased birds and killed them. They chased the squirrels, and when they could not capture them, they got long sturdy sticks and killed them. Finally they set a fire, which soon caused the forest to turn into a mass of flames. They stood at a distance and looked on.

The whole neighbourhood was trying to put out the fire, and no one paid any attention to Tom and Ted. Everybody was so busy fighting the fire that they were surprised when the parents of Tom and Ted frantically appealed to them to help them find the boys. They had not returned home. The people searched through the night but could not go into the woods because it was still very hot from the fire.

A week went by and there was still no sign of the boys. No one knew where they could have gone. Some of the neighbours remembered them standing with smirks on their faces, watching everyone trying to control the huge fire they had set. People stood around in groups, some of them whispering that the devil must have taken these boys, since no one else wanted them.

Finally the authorities were alerted, and they searched the boys' homes for clues. They found many articles which had been missing in the neighbourhood, but the parents could give no explanation. There were no excuses for these parents, who were supposed to provide guidance until such time as their offspring could guide and protect themselves.

While the forest fire had been burning furiously, Tom and Ted had seen a cat trying desperately to escape the flames. They had chased it and caught it and thrown it into the flames. To their surprise, the cat had walked through the flames unharmed.

Tom and Ted tried again and again to destroy the cat, but it was always unharmed. Enraged by their failure to destroy, they got a stick and pounded the cat. It fell to the ground, and as they looked on, the cat became all the helpless things they had destroyed. Birds, squirrels, cats, dogs and children were crying from the hurts these two boys had inflicted. Last of all, there were four loving hearts which had been broken by their own hands — the hearts of their parents.

As the boys stood almost petrified, the shape of the cat returned. It seemed to be dead at their feet, but suddenly it began to move. It rose from the ground, tall and straight. Before their very eyes, the cat had turned into a tall, graceful fairy with a magic wand.

The magic wand was lifted high as the fairy said, 'Tom and Ted, you shall feel every pain you have inflicted on creatures and human beings. You shall from now on be in the same category as the cats you have destroyed. You will never be able to utter a sound, you will hunt for your living and you will be hunted by other animals who are seeking revenge.

'You shall see your parents mourn. They, too, will have to answer for your misdeeds, for they have failed their responsibilities. With this magic wand I command you to become two cats to roam the woods.'

The two boys were never found and their parents continue to mourn for them.

WAYWARD EMILY

The old woman was a widow with two children, a boy and a girl. They lived in a cosy log house, with two rooms downstairs and two upstairs, set amidst tall pine trees on top of a hill. The religion of the family was the faith of the Onh-gwe-honh-weh (Indian).

The two children became adults. The young man did not stray from his faith and married a good woman of the same faith. However, the daughter was a wayward girl. Her mother was a good woman who had always stayed at home, but the daughter was restless and one day left the reservation to live on another Native settlement. For a long time her mother had no news from her.

One night someone knocked at the door. When the old lady opened it, she found her daughter standing there with a tiny baby in her arms. The girl was crying and asked for forgiveness. The mother asked her who the baby's mother was, and the daughter replied that the child was hers and the father had left her. The woman asked her in and told her to go to bed; they would talk in the morning.

In the morning Emily asked her mother if she would allow her to come home with her baby. It is difficult for a mother to turn her daughter away. She said Emily could come home under one condition — that she would take care of her baby and raise it as she herself had been raised. She must not have any liquor, as it was destroying her. Emily agreed to change her ways, and the three of them were very happy for four years.

One day Emily asked her mother if she would take care of the child while she went to visit her friends. Her mother refused, and one morning Emily was gone, leaving her baby behind.

Two years passed and Emily did not return home. Then one day she appeared. Two days later she gave birth to her second child.

Emily felt only hatred for her new baby. She even tried to kill her, so one of the neighbours took the baby away. Emily was completely out of her mind. She would run out of the house, and it would take three men to bring her back. On more than one occasion she tried to set fire to the house.

Gradually Emily seemed to change. She said she was sorry she had caused her mother so much heartache.

At night the old lady could hear her daughter talking to someone. Once she came down to see, but there was no one there. She thought that the girl might be worried about her baby but afraid to say anything to her. Then one night she heard the door and knew Emily had gone out. She did not expect her to come back, so she went to sleep.

In the morning when the woman went downstairs, her daughter was there. She said she had gone out with a man, who had given her a lot of money. The mother reminded her that she had promised to change her ways.

Every night Emily's screaming could be heard. When her mother ran down to her room, she could see that Emily was scared. She was looking everywhere and told her mother to lock the door, as the devil was coming after her. The old lady went to one of her neighbours and asked her to call the other neighbours to come to her house immediately. When the neighbours arrived, Emily was still screaming that the devil was at the door.

Someone called a minister, and he prayed for her. She said it was useless, as she had sold her soul to the devil; there was no escape for her. The kind minister continued praying until she quieted down and went to sleep. Large drops of sweat were on her face. Early in the morning she held the minister's hand, smiled and told him she was free.

Emily got well and after a few years she married a good man. However, it seemed she could not escape her fate. She began drinking again and drifted back to her wild life. One day while at a tavern, she fell down the stairs and died. Many people attended her funeral. Her body was not taken into the church but carried directly to the cemetery.

HE WAS LIKE AN ANIMAL

Even as a little baby he had been different, and no one had been able to understand him. When he was displeased he got a funny look in his eyes. Once he objected to his mother washing his face and jerked away from her. When she reached out for him, he bit her.

The mother told her husband of the boy's behaviour. She said she did not know what to do with him. She thought it was strange

that, although he was growing quickly, he did not try to talk. She wondered if he understood what she said to him. With tears in her eyes she said that their son looked and acted like an animal.

As time went on the boy grew bigger. He spent most of his time in the woods. He made sounds but uttered no words. His parents thought it would be better if they did not bother with him. Every day he came home for his meals, but often he stayed out all night. As long as he did not get into any trouble, they felt there was no need to worry.

One day in the woods a beautiful girl came up to the boy. She held out her hands to him. He just stared. She sat down beside him, but he paid no attention to her. The next day she returned. Again, she put out her hand. He almost smiled. The third time she came, he seemed to be expecting her. She sat down beside him and touched his face. She asked him if he could talk, and he shook his head. She stood up and began to climb up a tree. He watched her with a happy look on his face.

That night the boy took a bath and laid out clean clothes for the next day. His parents said nothing, but watching him they realized that something had aroused his interest.

He was up early the next morning and had breakfast with his parents. He watched his mother clear the table, then went up to her and touched her face. She smiled at him, and he smiled back at her. Looking happy, he went out and walked into the woods.

He went to the usual place and waited for his friend. He did not have to wait long before she arrived, dressed in pink and looking very pretty. She held out her hand, and as he was so clean she touched his shirt and said, 'Clean.' He smiled and nodded his head. He too said, 'Clean.' She was very happy and handed him a solid gold key. He took it and examined it. She took his hand and said, 'Follow me.' He went with her, carrying the key.

They went on and on and came to a stream of clear water. They followed the stream until they came to a bend. At this point the bank was quite steep. Motioning to him to follow, she skidded down

177

the bank and stood at the water's edge. She pointed to a door on the opposite bank. Taking hands, they waded across the river.

The girl motioned to him to use the gold key and unlock the door. As the door opened, they were blinded by the bright light coming from within. They heard music which sounded like turbulent waters. Suddenly, the music became calm, then slowly it grew clearer and louder. The boy who had been silent for so long now sang along with the music.

The good fairy had given the boy the golden key that opened the world to him and made him fully human.

THE KNOLL

There is a knoll on the Six Nations Reserve along the Grand River where the Little People dance on moonlight nights. Many people have seen the lights at this particular spot.

It was a Christmas Eve not long ago. In a house near the knoll a young woman was rocking a little child to sleep. Tears were streaming down her face, as unhappy memories came rushing back.

Hers had been a happy family. They had enjoyed the white man's religion with all its hopes of happiness. At Christmas there had been a Santa Claus to make the children happy, and plum pudding and roast turkey for dinner.

It had been on this night just a year ago that everything had come to an end. They had had a tree decorated to the top with Christmas lights, and the ten children in the home had gone to bed hoping that Santa would come with goodies and toys for them. In the morning Santa had come and gone — but their mother was gone also. She had cooked the dinner, and everything was in order, but she was gone. The emptiness of the home was more than the children could stand. The turkey did not taste right and the toys were not exciting. Their father spent his time outside, for the agony on his face was not for a merry Christmas day. The children asked for their mother, but he had no answers for them.

So again it was Christmas Eve. There were no tree to decorate and no turkey to roast. The younger children had gone to bed to wait for Santa Claus. Tears streamed down the girl's face as she thought of them and of her mother.

She looked out the window. Snow was falling softly on the hills nearby, where she had spent her childhood playing with her brothers and sisters. Suddenly she saw something else out there. Tiny lights were flickering among the snowflakes. As she watched them a feeling of peace came over her, and she turned from the window to go to bed. Pausing for a moment, she saw again in her mind's eye the beautiful tree that had stood in this room last Christmas Eve. Soon her young sisters and brothers would be scrambling down the stairs for their toys, and she could hardly bear to think of their disappointment.

The girl was awakened early the next morning by cries of delight from the children. She arose quickly and went downstairs. There, where it had always stood, was a beautiful Christmas tree, and underneath were presents piled high for every member of the family.

The children were happy with their toys. But what was to be done about their Christmas dinner? As she went into the kitchen, still dazed from the surprise of the tree, she found on the kitchen table everything they needed for their dinner, including a turkey to roast.

That evening, after the excitement of the day had died down and everyone had gone to bed, the girl sat down to think and look for some answers. Where had the tree and the food come from?

Just then, the kind lady who lived in the next house knocked at the door. The two women talked for a long time. The kind lady had come to help and comfort the young woman with all her responsibilities. She urged her never to forget that she was not alone. Her great-grandparents had been good people and had lived on that same property. They had found favour with the Little People. Near the house, she said, was a knoll upon which the Little

People danced and in time of sorrow or trouble found ways to help.

The girl remembered the lights she had seen the night before and went outside with her neighbour. With the snow falling tenderly and softly in the bright light of the moon, they slowly and reverently approached the knoll. They did not see the flicker of lights, only the prints of tiny feet, which made a circular path on top of the knoll.

The kind woman told the young girl that there is a fairy in every person's life, who can help him as long as he tries to be a good and uncomplaining person. 'Cry no more' is the rule of the fairies.

THE TRAIL

A young man working far from home heard some disturbing news, so he wrote to his father asking him about it.

In replying, his father said: 'Your best friend, George, went hunting and did not return. There was a search party, but no clues were found. Searching continued for one week. Then one of the men saw a man sitting under a tree. It was George, but he did not seem to recognize anyone. He was taken back to his home and family, but he did not remember them and kept saying "The trail to the open door," over and over. We do not know what to make of it.'

This young man, whose name was Andy, was greatly concerned. But he had a good job, and as long as his friend George was with his family, he would not worry.

At the end of the week he received another letter from his father, telling him that another man had disappeared. He too had gone hunting and not returned. The authorities were now warning people to stay away from the wooded area until they discovered what had happened to the second hunter. George was still in a semi-conscious state. When they told him about the other hunter, he just said 'The trail to the open door.'

The young man decided he would return home and see what he could do to clear up this mystery. He was certain the answer would be found if they located the trail to the open door. His father's house was near the wooded area. He knew and had covered every inch of that land and did not remember having seen a trail of any kind.

Andy reached his home just when the searchers were returning. His father was very glad to see him, as he was almost ill from exhaustion, searching for a clue to the mystery.

Andy went to see George. However, George did not recognize him, and there was nothing Andy could do to bring him back to reality. George just sat quietly, mumbling every now and again, 'The trail to the open door.' Andy encouraged him, saying to him, 'Let us talk about that trail to the open door.' George answered, 'No.' Andy asked for a pencil and paper. He drew a zigzag line, depicting a trail in the woods, and ended it at an open door. As George watched, Andy said, 'Come on, George; we will find the trail that leads to the open door.' Again George said, 'No.' Andy said good-bye to George and told him he would go alone to find the open door. George jumped up and yelled, 'No, you must not go alone; you will die. No, No.'

Andy told George's mother to alert the searchers to stay close by when they went into the forest but not to let George see them. Andy motioned to his friend, saying, 'Come on, George, let us find the trail to the open door.' George stood up and grabbed Andy's arm. They went out together, just as they had done many times in the past.

The two men walked for miles, deeper and deeper into the woods. Andy said to George, 'Let us play one of our old games and carve our initials on the trees.' Andy carved the letter 'A' and underneath it the letter 'G.' In this way, Andy was leaving a trail for the searchers to follow.

After they had gone some distance, George suddenly stopped. Looking worried, he pointed to the ground — he had found the trail. Andy cautioned him to be quiet while he stooped to the ground to examine what indeed looked like a trail. He detected a strange odour. He found some dead pine branches, and giving one to George and keeping one for himself, he set them alight and began to follow the trail.

George stopped, pointing ahead to the open door. Suddenly he remembered: Behind the door was a mad doctor, who enticed men into his den. He had many jars of animal brains, but now he needed human brains for his experiments. George could not remember how he himself had gotten out of this bizarre situation.

Just then they heard a piercing scream. George and Andy ran towards the open door, carrying their torches. Just inside was the mad doctor, struggling with the hunter who had disappeared. He was giving him a needle to paralyse him, but the hunter was strong and was fighting desperately for his life. Andy noticed again the odour he had been aware of outside. It was coming from the chemicals and decayed animal parts in the scientist's den.

George and Andy fought with the doctor and managed to make him release the hunter. Just then the searchers rushed in, grabbed the doctor and tied him securely. George and Andy helped the hunter to his home, and the mad doctor was handed over to the authorities. The mystery of the trail to the open door was solved, and the hunter had been rescued from a horrible death.

THE IVY-COVERED HOUSE

A couple owned a poultry farm on an Indian settlement along the Grand River. They sold fresh eggs and broilers, which provided them with a comfortable living throughout the entire year.

Their house was surrounded by tall pine and maple trees, and a nearby spring supplied a pond with fresh, clear water. Over the years, the family had grown and included two boys and a girl.

It was Christmas time on the farm. Fresh snow covered the ground, and ice sparkled on the pond. The children played all day and thought about the new skates Santa Claus might bring. It was their last happy Christmas together.

Shortly after the holiday season, the man noticed a number of changes in his home. His wife had changed and began complaining and arguing with her daughter. This was causing the girl to become unhappy and very nervous. She was losing weight and very rarely smiled at anyone. When anything went wrong in the house, her mother blamed her and punished her for it. Her brothers tried to protect her from their mother's anger, but it was no use.

One night after the children had gone to bed, the man had a talk with his wife. When he mentioned the daughter, his wife became very angry and told him she could not stand to have the girl around. After that he took the girl with him wherever he went, to protect her from her mother's wrath. Her brothers worried about her, and this only increased the bad atmosphere in the home.

It was Christmas Eve again. Though the mother would not allow a tree to be brought into the house, the boys went with their father and bought the little girl a cosy red sweater with matching red mitts. They wrapped the present in shiny paper and left it beside the fireplace, where she was sure to find it in the morning.

The little girl had kissed them goodnight and had gone to bed. Her mother screamed out to her to be up before dawn so she could help her cook the dinner. The girl answered, 'Yes, mother, I will.' The father was broken-hearted but did not know what to do. The boys were feeling unhappy too, so they went to bed as well.

Early in the morning the father made wood fires in the heaters to warm up the house. The mother came down with a scowl on her face and asked her husband why the girl had not come down. He told her she was too cruel to her only daughter and her behaviour had to stop. She began screaming for her daughter to come down at once, and this noise woke the boys, who ran to their sister's room to wake her.

The man and his wife were quarrelling furiously. Suddenly they heard the two boys calling their father to come upstairs. The parents ran upstairs and found their daughter lying in bed dead. The father took the boys away and went to get the doctor.

When the doctor came he told them the girl had been to see him on several occasions. She had talked to him and cried about the situation at home. She wanted to die because her mother hated her. Turning to the mother the doctor said, 'Now you can be happy, for you have killed your only daughter.'

Preparations were made for the child's funeral. After it was over, the brother who had tried most often to protect her was found dead beside the grave. Even before the boy's funeral was over, the father disappeared and was never seen again. The mother felt remorse, but it was too late to change anything.

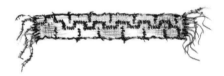

The years passed, and the remaining child left home. One day he returned and went to the cemetery. Standing by the graves of his sister and brother he cried out, 'Why am I left alone?'

He quickly went to his old home. Time had done many things. The roof was gone and the house was completely covered with ivy. Only one window still had glass in it. He drew closer and moved the ivy from the window. Inside he could see the same table and the clock still on the wall; even the rocking chair his father had once bought his mother was still there. But what a surprise! There she was, sitting in it! He stared, not believing this was really his mother. He saw a thin old woman, whose face showed much sadness.

The young man thought back to the two graves and remembered noticing fresh flowers. They could only have been left by his mother — the woman who had hated her daughter so much. He stood looking at his mother and remembered how she had destroyed their home with her hatred. He quickly turned and left the ivy-covered house forever.